DESTINY OF A NATION

How Prophets and Intercessors Can Mold History

D0166575

DESTINY OF A NATION

How Prophets and Intercessors Can Mold History

C. Peter Wagner, Editor

WAGNER
PUBLICATIONS

Destiny of a Nation
Copyright © 2001 by C. Peter Wagner
ISBN 1-58502-021-4

Published by
Wagner Publications
11005 N. Highway 83
Colorado Springs, Colorado 80921
www.wagnerpublications.org

Cover design by
Imagestudios
100 East St. Suite 105
Colorado Springs, CO 80903
719-578-0351

Interior design by Rebecca Sytsema

Rights for publishing this book in other languages are contracted by Gospel Literature International (GLINT). GLINT also provides technical help for the adaptation, translation, and publishing of Bible study resources and books in scores of languages worldwide. For further information, contact GLINT, P.O. Box 4060, Ontario, CA 91761-1003, USA. You may also send e-mail to glintint@aol.com, or visit their web site at www.glint.org.

1 2 3 4 5 6 7 8 9   07 06 05 04 03 02 01

CONTENTS

1. HISTORY BELONGS TO THE INTERCESSORS   7
   C. Peter Wagner

2. GOVERNMENTAL INTERCESSION   17
   Cindy Jacobs

3. THE "NUTCRACKER PROPHECY"   31
   Bart Pierce

4. HOW A PROPHET SEES GOVERNMENTAL   43
   CHANGE
   Chuck D. Pierce

5. SEALING TALLAHASSEE   59
   Bill Hamon

6. THE CALI-WEST PALM BEACH CONNECTION 67
   Héctor Torres

7. OPENING THE DOOR TO THE WHITE HOUSE   73
   Dutch Sheets

8. WHAT HAS BEEN GAINED BY INTERCESSION   85
   MUST BE MAINTAINED BY INTERCESSION
   Beth Alves

9. HOW TO PRAY THE FUTURE INTO BEING   93
   Chuck D. Pierce

   SUBJECT INDEX   102

Chapter One

History Belongs
to the Intercessors

C. Peter Wagner

An underlying presupposition of this book is that prayer can actually change things. Prayer to God can move His hand in such a way that the destiny of a whole nation can be determined through the ministry of intercessors and prophets.

This is, admittedly, a radical statement. How could it be possible that decisions and choices and actions of mere human beings might play a part in decisions, choices, and actions of an eternal, all-powerful, and sovereign God? Yet, the authors of this book believe that not only is such a thing possible, but that it actually happened in the United States presidential election of 2000.

Needed: A Certain Mindset

A certain mindset is needed in order to make sense out of the chapters that follow. The authors write with an unusual degree of passion and conviction because they were frontline participants in the spiritual drama surrounding the election of George W. Bush to the White House. All of them are recognized prophets and are members of the Apostolic Council of Prophetic Elders (ACPE). Most of them have an accompanying gift of intercession. One of the implications of operating in these gifts and ministries is that these individuals, and others like them, experience an extraordinary rapport with God. Consequently, they have first-hand knowledge, an inside track so to speak, of activities and intentions of spiritual beings, both in the supernatural realm of light and also in the darker world of malevolent, demonic spirits.

Thus, these authors "know" things that you do not hear on CNN, read about in *Time*, or deduce from polls. Scientific and humanistic mindsets may well write off the findings of this book as superstitions or fantasies of the imagination. Many would prefer to interpret events like elections through the lenses of recognized political scientists or credentialed social psychologists. Definable cause and effect to them would be what determines the destiny of a nation, not the supposed hand of God.

Tuning in to the Supernatural Dimension

Only a mindset in tune with the supernatural dimension of reality will be inclined to attribute Bush's victory to almighty God instead of to dimpled chads or to campaign finances or to Supreme Court justices. Is such a mindset legitimate?

In order to address that question, let's go back, for a moment, to our underlying presupposition that prayer can change things. Richard Foster says that when we pray, "We are working with God to determine the future. Certain things will happen in history if we pray rightly."[1] Walter Wink agrees. One of his most repeated quotes is, "History belongs to the intercessors,"[2] and I have used Wink's statement as the title of this chapter. Foster and Wink reflect the opinion of the overwhelming majority of biblical Christians who pray on a regular basis. They sincerely think that if they pray, certain things will happen, while if they don't pray other things are just as likely to happen.

Classical Evangelical Theism

Up to recently, most professional evangelical theologians merely tolerated such thinking as a somewhat unsophisticated, although relatively benign, conclusion of popular religion. Their classical theism postulated, rather, that the eternal God possessed absolute foreknowledge of everything that ever was going to happen. His overall purpose was going to be accomplished no matter what. The election of 2000? Before the foundation of the world, God had predestined that George W. Bush would win. Our prayers? According to many classical theologians with roots in Calvin and Augustine, our prayers would not substantially affect what God had already known beforehand. They could be seen as good, however, because our prayers may have changed us and thereby caused us to be more in tune with God's predetermined will.

The "Openness of God"

I said, "up to recently," because a momentous change is currently moving rapidly through the theological world. Termed the "openness of God," I would personally consider what is happening as the first time, at least in my memory, that professional theologians have actually helped lift the body of Christ to a strategic new level. Years ago, I found myself becoming less and less interested in professional theology, per se, because of its perennial disjunction from questions raised by practical ministry out in the field. But not openness theology. This now provides refreshing intellectual sophistication that undergirds the movements of prayer, strategic-level spiritual warfare, and prophetic intercession that have been developing over the past 30 years.

What is openness theology?

One of the first statements of this appealing theological mindset was a book, *The Openness of God* (InterVarsity Press) published in 1994 by a team of theological heavyweights: Clark Pinnock, Richard Rice, John Sanders, William Hasker, and David Basinger. A while later, Gregory Boyd of Bethel College in St. Paul, Minnesota, produced a 400-page (over 100 pages of them being fine-print footnotes) book, *God at War* (InterVarsity Press), defending what he terms a "warfare worldview." Boyd's book directly relates to what we have been experiencing in the field, and to the thrust of the book you hold in your hands on how prayer can literally mold the destiny of a nation.

GOD IS POWERFUL ENOUGH TO WIN ANY BATTLE, BUT HE HAS DESIGNED THINGS SO THAT THE RELEASE OF HIS POWER AT A GIVEN MOMENT OF TIME OFTEN IS CONTINGENT UPON THE DECISIONS AND THE ACTIONS OF HIS PEOPLE.

Gregory Boyd amasses convincing evidence that the biblical writers, both in the Old

Testament and in the New Testament, presuppose that "the good and evil, fortunate or unfortunate, aspects of life are to be interpreted largely as the result of good and evil, friendly or hostile, spirits warring against each other and against us."[3] This means that spiritual warfare is really war. It is not a divine charade with the outcome predetermined by God no matter what. God's purpose may be thwarted or it may be accomplished depending, to one degree or another, on the obedience of His people and their willingness to use the weapons of spiritual warfare that He has provided. God is powerful enough to win any battle, but He has designed things so that the release of His power at a given moment of time often is contingent upon the decisions and the actions of His people.

Does God Control Everything That Happens?

A principal weapon of spiritual warfare is prayer. Not just routine or mediocre prayer, but prayer powerful enough to move God's hand in order to determine the destiny of a whole nation. Openness theologians teach that "God, in grace, grants humans significant freedom to cooperate with or work against God's will for their lives, and he enters into dynamic, give-and-take relationships with us. . . . Sometimes God alone decides how to accomplish these goals. On other occasions, God works with human decisions, adapting his own plans to fit the changing situation. *God does not control everything that happens*. Rather, he is open to receiving input from his creatures. In loving dialogue, God invites us to participate with him to bring the future into being"[4] (italics mine).

This is precisely the mindset that guides this book and its authors. They agree with John Sanders who says, "Our prayers can have an effect on God's plans. It makes no sense to say God grieves, changes his mind, and is influenced by our prayers, and also claim that God tightly controls everything so that everything that occurs is what God desires to happen!"[5] Our premise is that God desired that George W. Bush be elected president of the United States in 2000. However, the opposing forces obviously desired otherwise, and a battle for the election was taking place in the heavenlies. The outcome was not a foregone conclusion, but in this case God's people on earth moved together in gifts of prophecy and intercession to the extent that God's Plan A materialized and the destiny of our nation for the next 40 years was determined.

God is Not a Republican

Having said that, let me establish the fact that this book is not a political statement. George Bush happens to be a Republican, but these authors are not defending the Republican Party. Neither is this a statement that George W. Bush should be seen as a favored servant of God while Al Gore should be seen as an ominous servant of darkness. Both men, in fact, profess to know God and to be born-again Christians, and their public lives would not indicate otherwise. Many born-again Christians voted Democrat while others voted Republican. God is not a Republican. A Democratic vote was not an endorsement of the demonic, it was simply an expression of an informed personal opinion in a free society. It would be foolish to suppose that God's choice of George W. Bush would have been based on the notion that he had gained more heavenly Brownie points over the years than Al Gore. No. It did not have as much to do with the individuals, much less the political parties, as it did with the future direction of the United States.

Who Recognizes Prophets?

A while ago I stated that the authors of this book were recognized prophets. I know that many readers will have raised a question relating to how this happens. Who makes a person a prophet? Who recognizes the prophets? How can we tell the difference between a true prophet and a false prophet?

These are vital questions. In fact, the authenticity of this book depends on the answers to them. Is it really possible that, in the year 2000, some individuals knew with a considerably higher degree of certainty than most others that God's choice for president would be George W. Bush? I, for one, think it is possible for the simple reason that I believe in the gift and office of prophecy.

Prophets in the Foundation of the Church

Part of the mindset needed to understand this book is based on our belief in Ephesians 4:11: "[Jesus] Himself gave some to be apostles, some prophets, some evangelists, and some pastors and teachers." This was not something temporary that lasted only a century or two. These gifted individuals would be necessary "until we all come to the unity of the faith and the knowledge of the Son of God, to a perfect man, to the measure of the stature of the fullness of Christ" (Eph. 4:13).

Prophets, yesterday and today, are vital to the accomplishment of God's Plan A for our lives. The Bible says, "Surely the Lord God does nothing unless he reveals His secret to His servants the prophets" (Amos 3:7). It also says, "Believe in the Lord your God, and you shall be established; believe His prophets, and you shall prosper" (2 Chron. 20:20). No wonder the apostle Paul affirmed that the church is "built on the foundation of the apostles and prophets, Jesus Christ Himself being the chief cornerstone" (Eph. 2:20).

The Gift and Office of Prophet

How does a certain believer become a prophet? God makes the choice, just as He does with pastors or administrators or teachers or those with the gift of healing or service or teaching or hospitality. He decides what spiritual gifts He will give each of us, and these gifts determine how we are supposed to function as members of the body of Christ. One of the gifts is the gift of prophecy. There can be no legitimate prophet who has not first received the spiritual gift of prophecy from God.

But receiving the gift is only a first step. Being recognized as having the *office* of prophet is the second step. This is a bit more fuzzy to many because our churches in general have not been accustomed to recognizing individuals as prophets. For centuries we have been ordaining individuals as pastors, signifying our public recognition that they have the gift of pastor. But it has only been within the past twenty years or so that a similar thing is being applied to prophets. We are still in the process of agreeing on a protocol.

The Apostolic Council of Prophetic Elders

Part of this process has been the establishment of the Apostolic Council of Prophetic Elders (ACPE). As the ministry of prophets has expanded, a number of mistakes have been made. Some prophets, in their enthusiasm over actually hearing from God and knowing His will for certain situations, have ended up making a nuisance of themselves. Some have offended pastors and apostles and believers in general. One of the most frequent and persistent criticisms of prophets is that they have not held themselves accountable to anyone.

The more mature and responsible prophets have taken this call for accountability seriously. While some of them do maintain meaningful accountability to pastors or apostles or other Christian leaders, they also feel that prophets should hold themselves accountable to other prophets. A group of around twenty-five of these prophets have formed the ACPE, over which I preside as a convening apostle. We meet together on a regular basis in order to develop personal relationships from which flows mutual accountability.

Throughout the election year of 2000, a general consensus within ACPE developed that the Holy Spirit was speaking strongly to the church in America about the election. Since the Supreme Court removed prayer from the schools 40 years ago, the moral fiber of our nation has been unraveling at an alarming rate. Prophets began hearing from God that the election of 2000 would set the course for the next 40 years. The election was so important that it could either perpetuate the downward spiral or it could turn the nation around.

A Red Alert

Experienced prophets and intercessors moved into a red alert mode. An infrastructure, the U.S. Strategic Prayer Network, had been developed as the result of a decade of mobilizing intercessors. Strong leadership nationally and in each state was in place. Sophisticated electronic communications were up and running. Prophets had connected with each other in an accountability network. The firsthand story of how this massive activation of prophets and intercessors took place is told in this book.

I would not suppose that the election of 2000 was the only U.S. election that was ever determined, to one extent or another, by serious, powerful prayer. But, to my knowledge, no other such case has been documented this well. Reminiscent of the documentation of Rees Howell's intercession during World War II, I am confident that *Destiny of a Nation* will help raise the water level of faith in the efficacy of prayer and intercession throughout our country.

Notes

[1] Richard Foster, *Celebration of Discipline* (San Francisco: HarperSanFrancisco, 1988), p. 35.
[2] Walter Wink, *Engaging the Powers* (Minneapolis MN: Fortress Press, 1992), p. 298.
[3] Gregory A. Boyd, *God at War* (Downers Grove IL: InterVarsity Press, 1997), p. 13.
[4] Clark Pinnock, Richard Rice, John Sanders, William Hasker, David Basinger, *The Openness of God* (Downers Grove IL: InterVarsity Press, 1994), p. 7.
[5] John Sanders, "Does God Know Your Next Move?" *Christianity Today*, June 11, 2001, p. 52.

Governmental Intercession

Cindy Jacobs

Cindy Jacobs is an ordained minister and is president and co-founder (along with her husband, Mike) of Generals of Intercession which is a missionary organization devoted to training in the area of prayer and spiritual warfare. Cindy also serves as the coordinator for the U.S. Strategic Prayer Network, a network of ministry leaders who strategize for the  United States on the spiritual warfare prayer level, seeking national revival.

The United States of America held a crucial presidential election in the year 2000. During that season, the Lord shifted the body of Christ in America into a new level of intercessory prayer. It is true that intercessors pray regularly for those in government. But this time, a quantifiable new anointing came upon the body of Christ with the assignment to unlock the will of God over the nation.

"Governmental Intercession"

This new thrust that we now speak of as "governmental intercession" brought us into a new understanding of the Scripture in 1 Timothy 2:1-3: "Therefore I exhort first of all that supplications, prayers, intercessions, and giving of thanks be made for all men, for kings, and all who are in authority, that we may lead a quiet and peaceable life in all godliness and reverence. For this is good and acceptable in the sight of God our Savior."

The circle of intercessors that I move in understood from the very beginning of the electoral process that we were not to pray in a partisan manner, but rather we were to seek the Lord for His perfect will for the nation. In order to do this, we prayed and asked God to help us discern which candidate would be most likely to swing our nation toward a more biblical worldview. It didn't matter to us whether they wore the label "Democrat" or "Republican." There are many godly Democrats and many liberal Republicans who are pro-abortion and stand for other anti-biblical stances as well. What mattered to us was finding out whom God had chosen.

Another thing that we came to realize as we progressed with the electoral process was that it is one thing to know the will of God and to hear a word concerning His perfect will, and yet another thing for His will to come to pass. In other words, there are many things that happen in this world, but they are not God's will, because His children simply do not respond properly and stand in the gap. "I sought for a man among them who would make a wall, and stand in the gap before Me on behalf of the land, that I should not destroy it; but I found no one" (Ezek. 22:30).

The Prophets Agree

This was actually a topic of discussion in the meeting of the Apostolic Council of Prophetic Elders (ACPE) during the aftermath of November 7, 2000, the day when the nation voted on the presidency. We asked ourselves, "Why have we had such a hard time giving a prophetic word concerning who would be the next president? Why wasn't it more clear?"

This was particularly pressing because we all felt we had received a clear word that God's choice for president was George W. Bush. However, while we agreed that this was God's will, to a person we had been reluctant to prophesy that in public. We were not sure why we all felt that way. However, the moment that we collectively realized that we had independently come to the same conclusion,

FOR TOO LONG WE HAVE COMPLAINED ABOUT THE CONDITION OF THE NATION WITHOUT FIGHTING TO SAVE IT THROUGH PRAYER AND BECOMING INVOLVED.

something shifted in our midst and we immediately went to battle on a prophetic level that I have rarely experienced. God literally showed us how to unlock those things that had previously been tied up in the heavenlies over the election.

Several prayed powerful prayers of identificational repentance. One of the prophets from Florida, for example, was able to stand in the gap for the sins of his state. This was crucial because Florida had become the deciding state for the election. Rarely have I seen such prophetic agreement turning into a literal "counsel of the Lord." We were standing before the throne in perfect harmony in a time of dire national need.

At the end of our intense prayer time, we knew that God would answer those prayers. We also knew there was more to be done, but we had made major headway into releasing the will of God into the earth from heaven, as we are told to do in Matthew 6:10.

The Courts Will Decide!

We also know that God will do nothing without first telling His servants, the prophets (see Amos 3:7). In addition to this time of prophetic breakthrough in the ACPE meeting, God had spoken to a number of people to pray at the courthouses and for the judicial system long before the decision surrounding a recount by the Florida Supreme Court. There was a certain timeframe allotted for possible recounting, and the Florida Supreme Court in Tallahassee made a decision concerning it that was contested before the United States Supreme Court.

A year and a half before this, the Lord had led me to preach a message entitled, "The Court is in Session," that called for prayer for the Supreme Court of the land. Through what God had revealed to me for the message, I had known that the election decision would end up with the court system. In fact, over a number of months I had shared publicly that I felt that the next U.S. election would ultimately be decided by the courts.

I preached this message for a Global Harvest Ministries

conference Peter Wagner sponsored. The text was taken from the powerful passage found in Daniel 7:9-10: "I watched till thrones were put in place, and the Ancient of Days was seated; His garment was white as snow, and the hair of His head was like pure wool. His throne was a fiery flame, its wheels a burning fire: A fiery stream issued and came forth from before Him; ten thousand times ten thousand stood before Him. *The court was seated, and the books were opened*" (italics added).

The prophetic essence of that message was (and is) that we needed to pray so that the thrones of God would be put in place, convening the court of heaven through intercessory prayer, so that the will of God would be done in the United States of America. We were to essentially pray and stand until *His* law became *the* law of the land.

Spreading Across
the Fifty States

Part of the strategy to make this happen was to have the intercessors attached to the US Strategic Prayer Network (USSPN) pray at different carefully-selected idolatrous sites in all fifty states on November 4, just prior to the election. Little did we realize at the time how important and strategic that intercession would become! The destiny of a nation hung in the balance!

Working in conjunction with Ron and Darla Campbell, and Christian Bass of The Jeremiah Project, we launched prayer in all fifty states at sites chosen by the prayer network leaders. This project was carried out quietly and efficiently. The prayer warriors were trained as spiritual SWAT teams. They all hit their targets on the same day! To our knowledge there has not been a single bit of backlash from the enemy toward any of those who participated in these strategic prayer times on November 4.

Of course, this was not all the prayer that had preceded the election. Many others such as the National Prayer Committee, Intercessors for America, and similar groups had also been praying intensely. More directly related to this book, intercessors from the USSPN[1] and Bill Hamon's Christian International had gone to Tallahassee, Florida led primarily by Chuck Pierce and Martha Lucia. Bill Hamon details this story in a later chapter.

Mobilizing Florida's USSPN

On several occasions, Diane Buker, the Florida USSPN Coordinator, took teams to pray at the Florida state courthouse. In fact, I had previously instructed the whole USSPN to focus prayer on the court system during the elections. Even without knowing how crucial their state would become, the Florida intercessors heeded the word and sent out numbers of powerful prayer teams.

During the time of our national turmoil arising from the fact that our election had not been decided on election day, our Florida state intercessors really stepped up to the plate. One of the cities at the vortex of the election controversy was West Palm Beach. In studying the spiritual mapping that had been done in that city, the intercessors discovered that one reason there was such a swirling around West Palm Beach could be that it was one of the cities that had refused asylum to the 900-plus German Jews fleeing Hitler right before the outbreak of World War II.[2] With this knowledge of how to target their intercession, USSPN teams fervently prayed to unlock the will of God over West Palm Beach.

Deploying the
Prophetic Intercessors

On November 8, the day after the election, the Florida Supreme Court ruled that the ballots in all 67 counties would be
recounted. By then it had become clear that Florida held the
swing vote. If Florida's electoral votes went to Al Gore, he
would be the next president. If they went to George W. Bush,
he would sit in the White House. Early in the morning of
November 9, the Lord spoke directly to Diane Buker that many
of the gates (or places where God desired to make His will
known in Florida) had been closed for various reasons. He
told her that the intercessors needed to stand in the gap and
pray that Jesus would have new liberty to come into their state
at every level. Within the course of two hours, through their
well-honed system of communication, they had contacted 90%
of their state and asked them to send our prophetic intercessory teams immediately.

Diane asked the teams to address Florida's territorial, governmental, financial, and media gates—commanding them to
open and inviting in the King of Glory.[3] After that time they
based their prayers on Zechariah 8:16, "Speak each man the
truth to his neighbor; give judgment in your gates for truth,
justice, and peace." Diane asked the intercessors to call for
justice, and to plead for truth in the election process and in the
state.

The Slave Block
in St. Augustine

In addition to those teams, Diane Buker herself took a team to

St. Augustine, Florida. St. Augustine is the oldest permanent city in the nation. They had received a word that St. Augustine was the gate to our whole nation, and that they were to go there and pray. As they made the trip, they asked the Lord where they should go, knowing that this would involve high-level spiritual warfare. They all agreed that God was assigning them to pray on the first slave block in America. They actually stood on top of the slave block to pray and proclaim! Here is the prophecy they received at that time: "If the church of this nation doesn't press in during this time, as a country we are in danger of falling into the hands of wicked masters and be given over to slavery as a nation."

Let me explain a bit about prophetic activity. It isn't enough to simply receive the word of the Lord. God's servants must follow through into a second dimension of the prophetic and ask God for His divinely-ordered strategy as to how to fulfill the conditions of the prophecy. In this case, that would mean seeking the Lord about the exact nature of the intercession that would shift the nation governmentally in order to avert the judgment of being given over to slavery. This would include searching Scripture as well as identificational repentance,[4] and then interceding in such a way as to prevent the judgment from coming to the nation.

God is the Judge

The Lord gave the prayer team in St. Augustine the same three Scriptures that were used at the other sites (Ps. 24:7-10, Zech. 8:16, and Is. 29:4). He also gave them a fourth Scripture found in Psalm 75:6-7: "For exaltation comes neither from the east nor from the west nor from the south. But God is the Judge: He puts down one and exalts another."

There are times when you are deep in intercession and

suddenly you feel a joy and release in your heart. You then know that the heavens have opened up and God's answer is being released into the earth. The battle over the powers of darkness trying to stop God's will is finished! This was the case as the Florida intercessors completed the prophetic path that God had assigned them to walk in intercessory prayer. *Within an hour of completing their prayer assignment in St. Augustine, the news media reported that the U.S. Supreme Court had overruled the Florida Supreme Court's decision to recount Florida's ballots by hand!*

For those who may not understand this kind of governmental intercession, it might sound strange when I say that there was a battle over releasing the will of God into the earth. Isn't God's will automatic? Not always! If you will think with me about a passage in the book of Daniel, it may become clearer to you.

Daniel (whose name means "God is my Judge") had set his face toward God with fasting and prayer to seek an answer from God. He fasted for three weeks. His fast included abstaining from personal hygiene in addition to being without food. I can only imagine what he must have looked like at this point! But it was then that God sent an angel to Daniel to help him understand the vision he had been given:

God's Will is Not Automatic

The angel told Daniel that he was greatly beloved of God (don't we all want to hear that from Him?), and that the angel was there to help him understand. The following Scripture is powerful: "Then he said to me, 'Do not fear, Daniel, for from the first day that you set your heart to understand, and to humble yourself before your God, your words were heard; and I have come because of your words. But the prince of the kingdom of Persia withstood me twenty-one days; and behold, Michael, one of the chief princes, came to help me, for I had been left alone there with the kings of Persia'" (Daniel 10:12-13).

This leads me to the principle that God's plan is frequently to accomplish His will through the prayers of His people on the earth. His will is not automatic, but in many cases it can only be implemented through intercessory prayer. We must not take a "live and let live" or "que será, será" attitude.

I like these words attributed to Edmund Burke (1729-1797): "The only thing necessary for the triumph of evil is for good men to do nothing. Nobody made a greater mistake than he who did nothing because he could only do a little."

Our Prayers Count!

One trap that some fall into is feeling that their prayers don't count. Nothing could be further from the truth! Every prayer touches heaven when it is done according to God's will. We all need to pray and teach our children to pray for many things, but especially for our government.

God is teaching those of us in the prayer movements here in the United States that if our government moves out of line with the will of God, we can begin to shift the nation back where it belongs through governmental intercession. For too long we have complained about the condition of the nation without fighting to save it through prayer and becoming involved.

Dangers of Prayerlessness

In the year prior to the election of 2000, the Lord gave a prophecy to Dutch Sheets that said in essence that the Lord wasn't pleased with our prayerlessness for the president, namely for Bill Clinton. This didn't mean that no one prayed because there were at that time and still are dedicated prayer groups in Washington D.C. who have labored tirelessly in governmental intercession. However, as a whole, most Christians were not praying for their leaders as they should have. I believe that Dutch's prophecy was a hinge word to wake up the nation to pray for those in government.

As I traveled around the nation and shared this word, I certainly found that too many of us were guilty of prayerlessness concerning those in authority over us. A great wave of repentance subsequently hit the church over our lack of obedience to the Scripture that I began this chapter with: 1 Timothy 2:1-3.

What transpires over the next few years in this nation will determine the course of the United States for many years to come. It will affect our children and our children's children. We must take the lessons learned over the past few years and press toward the mark of establishing this nation once again according to the plumb line of our national motto, "One Nation Under God." We repeat this motto every time we pledge allegiance to the flag: ". . . one nation under God, indivisible, with liberty and justice for all."

Remaining "One Nation Under God"

This nation will only be indivisible while we remain under God. The enemy is at the gate. There are enemies within and without. Our children can no longer pray out loud over a microphone and use the most precious name in heaven and earth, the name of Jesus Christ. There is no other God but Him. His name is not Buddha or Allah or Shiva. This nation, like any nation, needs a Savior and only His laws can establish our nation in righteousness.

I am convinced that this message of governmental intercession is one of the most important ones we can teach the church today. The soul of our nation is at stake. We have pressed through with the beginnings of establishing His will on the earth. The believers of America must not stop praying until prayer is put back in school *in the Name of Jesus*. There is no other name, not in heaven or earth, wherein our nation or we can be saved. We must fight in the heavenlies to put Bible reading, the establishment of the plumb line of God's word back into our schools.

The Bible says that righteousness exalts a nation (see Prov. 14:34). Therefore we must press into prayer to shift this nation to become the city set on a hill dreamed about and prayed for by our forbearers. We must do this not only for our children, but also for the generations who will come after us and inherit the land.

I Have a Dream

I have a dream that one day sins such as racism, abortion, sexual promiscuity, and others, which grieve the heart of God, will be abolished in this nation. In my dream my little grandson, Malachi Jude, is reaching into his school desk for a little black book with the words, Holy Bible, stamped in gold on the cover to begin his first day of school. I see him in a classroom filled with little boys and girls of many different races who love each other and love God. In my vision I can see them bow their heads together and begin to pray, *"Our Father, who art in heaven, hallowed be Thy Name,*

Your Kingdom come, Your will be done on earth, as it is in heaven."

Notes

[1] The U.S. Strategic Prayer Network (USSPN) covers all fifty states, divided into eight regions. Many of the states have their own state regions as well. For instance, as of this writing, Florida has 54 coordinators within the state in addition to their state coordinator, Diane Buker. C. Peter Wagner is the head of the International Strategic Prayer Network as International Apostle. Cindy Jacobs serves as National Apostle for USSPN and Chuck Pierce serves as Mobilizing Apostle. In addition, Brian Kooiman assists Chuck Pierce in administration and communication. For information on the network contact Brian Kooiman at usspn@globalharvest.org. You may also log onto www.generals.org for further information.

[2] Not long ago I personally journeyed to a reconciliation meeting with the survivors of the St. Louis at a meeting sponsored by Tom Hess and Progressive Vision in Ft. Lauderdale. The St. Louis is the steamship which carried the Jewish refugees. It was quite touching as we met with 68 Jews, including some of the survivors. Most of those turned away from West Palm Beach were given asylum in Europe and later died in the Holocaust. This was a very moving time as I talked to the survivors, and looked at pictures of their relatives and loved ones. As we gazed at the photographs they would murmur in answer to my inquiry as to what happened to their family. Many would say, "Oh, my mother and father died in a concentration camp." I will be forever touched by meeting these brave Jewish survivors of the St. Louis.

[3] For more information and understanding on this kind of prophetic intercession please read my book *Possessing the Gates of the Enemy* (Chosen Books).

[4] For a good understanding of the subject of identificational repentance, an excellent source is *Healing America's Wounds* (Regal Books) by John Dawson.

Chapter Three

The "Nutcracker Prophecy"

Bart Pierce

Bart Pierce serves as senior pastor of Rock City Church in Baltimore, Maryland, which has experienced a mighty outpouring of God's presence since January, 1997. People from all over the country and abroad travel to attend the revival meetings held every Monday and Tuesday night. In addition, Bart also provides apostolic  oversight to churches in the Ukraine, Madagascar, and the United States, and has a passion for seeing the body of Christ unite together.

Our story, like the other chapters in this book, is a continual prophetic thread, a tapestry of sovereign revelation of God's plan to heal our nation. At Rock City Church in Baltimore, Maryland we'd been blessed with powerful, revival-type services for a little over two years when, on April 14, 1999, a sovereign, God-orchestrated meeting took us almost by surprise.

But first a bit of background.

A "Breaker Anointing"

For some time Rock City Church had been recognized as being gifted with a "breaker anointing." One such notable breakthrough took place on January 19, 1997, when God suddenly came in the midst of our church in a great explosion of His manifest presence. We experienced Him filling every area of our lives and our church. Now even our city has been measurably affected. Tommy Tenney came in every Monday and Tuesday night for three and a half years to be a part of these meetings.

The series of events that I'm about to describe, I believe, are part of a great prophetic destiny. God desired to see a new, born-again president elected, and our nation changed.

It all happened during a Spiritual Warfare Conference, which we were hosting at our church. The meeting that occurred that memorable night turned out to be vital to the destiny of our nation and to the incredible events that took place as the election of 2000 unfolded. That night none of us foresaw the great impact the move of God would have on shaping the course of the prophetic events that were coming to change our nation.

Rick Ridings Prophesies

Our coming together was a direct result of a prophecy that was given the prior year (February 16, 1998) by Rick Ridings, a fellow member of the Apostolic Council of Prophetic Elders, regarding Washington, D.C. Once we received the prophecy, it was distributed throughout Baltimore to area pastors, and it was also given to Ron Johnson

of Bethel Temple, in Hampton, Virginia. The word reso-
nated with us, and we began to move forward with prayer,
rallying intercessors, and connecting churches. Rick had
come to our church several times for our 'revival services,
but he was not able to be in the service this particular April
night, so we read the prophetic word that God had given
him to the congregation.

We now refer to this as "The Nutcracker Prophecy":

"I felt the Lord saying that this is a very strategic time
for the 'digging of wells' not only in specific congregations, but also for certain cities and regions. For the past
year, God has been speaking to me through Genesis 26,
where Isaac re-opened the old wells of his father Abraham,
which had been stopped up by the Philistines. But it was
also a time of digging new wells. This is such a time.

A "Spiritual Nutcracker"

"I felt the Lord saying that He has His eye on Washington,
D.C. at this time. In His sovereign plan, He has been preparing a 'spiritual nutcracker' which is being formed by
what He is doing in Maryland and Virginia. His heart is to
bring spiritual pressure from the two sides of this nutcracker
to break open the 'hard shell' of Washington, D.C.

"To form this nutcracker, God has been opening ancient wells in Maryland and Virginia, in areas which have
known true spiritual awakenings in the past. Although He
is re-opening wells in many churches and cities in these
states, there are two wells which have been re-opened to
the point that they are beginning to tap into artesian springs
which will soon result in large numbers coming to the Lord.
These two wells are in Baltimore, Maryland, and in the

Tidewater area of Virginia. I sensed that the focal points of this particular well digging were in the Rock Church in Baltimore, and Bethel Temple in Hampton, Virginia. I felt He said that the intercessors in these two churches and cities are to not only continue to dig down locally, but also to tunnel through to Washington, D.C. When the tunnels from Maryland and Virginia meet each other in Washington, then a new well will spring up in that desert.

"It is absolutely vital for us all to remember that these tunnels cannot be dug by any prayers of pride and arrogance, or by judgment and accusation toward Washington or its politicians. They will only be dug by those praying in humility and repentance. To those in these surrounding states the Lord says not to fear that the tunneling toward Washington will somehow be a distraction. It is actually this tunneling sideways that will release the tunneling locally to go deeper more quickly and to tap into those artesian wells that will release the work of the Holy Spirit for the harvest."

The Beginning
of the Breakthrough

Nearly two thousand people from up and down the eastern Seaboard had come to the service that night, as well as people from many congregations around Baltimore. We came to make a declaration that now was the time for the hard shell of Washington to break open.

I began to pray, "God, from Virginia to Washington, D.C.—from Hampton to Baltimore—we have gathered for a purpose. We have gathered to glorify You and to call upon Your name. We have called on Your name, that Your ear would be inclined to Your children. Let the heavens come a little lower tonight. Let the earth begin to cry out, as the prophet Hosea said. Let there be a cry that comes out of this earth till heaven and earth kiss each other. Father we thank You."

Then we softly sang: "Lord, You have favored Your land, and covered the sin of Your people. You have taken away all Your wrath, now turn us, oh God, once again. Cause Your anger to cease and revive us again. Show us Your mercy, oh Lord. Grant us salvation and speak peace to Your saints, that glory may dwell in Your land. Let the heavens come down and kiss the earth; let glory rush in and bring new birth. And truth shall spring out of the earth, and righteousness shall look down from heaven."

Three Prophetic Leaders Confirm the Nutcracker Breakthrough

Remarkably, three nationally-known prophetic leaders were present at the service, each of whom found himself playing a key role in the unfolding of divine events. They were Tommy Tenney, Lou Engle, and Dutch Sheets.

First, Tommy Tenney, also an ACPE member, came forward and began to pray, "Lord, we know from history that as the king goes, so goes the nation. We have no king, but the central focus of our government is in a city. It's a city that has been wrought with problems, and we do not stand in judgment against that—we cry for mercy for that. For every child whose blood has run in the streets of that city, their blood is crying now to heaven for mercy. We stand against the forces of violence and we cry for the force of grace. Let the fire from heaven fall. Now Lord, we have no right to pray for the fire to fall if we're not willing to be fuel for the fire. We lay ourselves on the altar. Consume us, and may the fire of God fall! Consume us, and the cities we're now in, to the glory of God the Father!"

Three Pastors Form the Points of the Nutcracker

At that point, two other pastors joined me in the platform. I represented one handle of the nutcracker and Ron Johnson from Hampton, Virginia, represented the other. Dennis Pisani, a pastor of Glory Tabernacle in Washington D.C., represented the nut to be cracked, so to speak.

Tommy Tenney continued: "We know there are many representatives here tonight, but we have chosen just one from each place. There's something about the power of human words. Human words are the only thing on earth that are presently in heaven. They are the only thing that God collects and treasures. He collects them in a vial and He puts them there because our words are powerful. God said to Hosea, 'Come at Me with your words.' What we are doing here tonight is collectively coming together with our words. I'm going to add my words to your words; you're going to add your words to your neighbor's words, and we're going to throw them toward heaven for God to collect them up. Earthly words cause earthly actions. If we do, God will show up and crack the hard shell!"

Ron Johnson then prayed, "Lord, You said there would come a time. We believe we're in that time. We believe this is the beginning of where we are to cry out, 'Spring up, oh well!' This is the beginning, where the hard shell around Washington shall be broken. We thank you that the wall is coming down and the glory of the Lord is coming in. Sweep in, oh glory of the Lord! Come, take over, and be exalted, oh God!"

Dennis Pisani began to share, "As we stood in Immanuel's Church (Silver Springs, Maryland) Sunday night, we spoke out a declaration, and I just want to repeat it and release it here tonight. I speak to Maryland and I speak to Washington and I speak to Virginia. A three-fold cord shall never be broken again. From the north, the east, the south, and the west... revival, revival, revival! Come, revival, come!"

As a prophetic act, I then grabbed hold of a large ceramic nut in one hand and a hammer in the other and cracked it wide open. A deafening victory shout went forth throughout the sanctuary.

The Prophetic Offering

At that point there was a collective witness to take up an offering for Washington, as a seed offering. The former Mayor of Washington, Marion Barry, and his wife, Cora, were seated on the front row. While I hadn't known they were coming that evening, I had met them previously. In fact, Cora Masters Barry had recently visited the church with some friends of hers, to learn about our Ministries of Compassion work. We asked the Barrys if they would receive the offering for Washington, and they agreed, but "Only for the children." Cora Masters Barry has a tremendous heart for the children, and she has a great outreach ministry to the children of D.C.

Tommy Tenney began to pray: "We bless this offering. May it repair every breach, may it repair every gap in the hedge, and may it send missiles of mercy into the cesspools of sin. Let the light of the glory of God break out into places of darkness, that where sin would abound, grace would much greater abound."

Lou Engle and the Elijah Prayer

I believe that we are living in the day when the Elijah Prayer is coming to pass, when the hearts of the fathers are being turned to the children. There was more going on in that service than any of us knew. This became apparent, as Lou Engle

THE BODY OF CHRIST CAME TO A NEW LEVEL OF PROPHETIC INTERCESSION IN THIS SEASON, AND CONSEQUENTLY THE FUTURE LOOKS BRIGHT FOR OUR NATION!

of Harvest Rock Church in Pasadena, California, was invited to the platform. Who could have guessed that this evening would also be a breakthrough night for the birthing of what would be "The Call D.C."?

Lou began to share, "One and a half years ago I prophesied that a million kids would come to the Mall in D.C., on the heels of the Promise Keepers.   God wants to restore the hearts of the children to the fathers. I began to prophesy that a million kids would come, cry out to God, and fast and pray for a great turn around in America. This past week a lady walked up to me and asked me if I'd ever had a vision of putting a million kids together on the Mall in Washington. I said, 'As a matter of fact, I've actually spoken that it will come forth.' She said that she had one hundred thousand dollars to sow as seed money to that end.

"Two days later I met Rick Ridings, whom I'd never met

before. He said that I needed to see Bart Pierce, whom I had not met either. Later, I came out to the East Coast with my family for a wedding, and I was invited to speak in Philadelphia at Jack Hanley's church. Jack told me that two days prior he had been with Bart Pierce and when Bart heard that I was preaching in his church, he said, 'I need to speak to Lou Engle.' I had no idea that I'd have an appointment with Bart Pierce, or that this meeting was going on tonight.

"I told Bart that I believed God wanted to put a million kids on the Mall of Washington, D.C. He said, 'Lou, I helped put 500,000 kids on the Mall in 1988 in Washington for Jesus, and I sense something like that is going on now.' This is a prophetic hour to break the power of Jezebel in the land and release the Elijah anointing—for a million kids to cry out to God for a turn around in our nation!"

Dutch Sheets and the Destiny of a Nation

Dutch Sheets, pastor of Springs Harvest Fellowship in Colorado Springs, took the microphone next and started off by saying, "You don't have to be very prophetic to sense the destiny of the Lord in this place and for this time and for this season. I don't want to be overly dramatic, but I feel very safe in saying what God is doing and what He is going to do. The destiny of a nation hangs in the balance! Holy Spirit, we ask you to take our words tonight and be carried throughout the nation. May what takes place in this room tonight rock the nation. We have no faith in our ability to do that but we have all the faith that we need that You can do it.

"I'm going tell you about a journey that God has had me on for several years. God gave me a vision in 1991, as I was speaking in Spokane, Washington. Suddenly, with my eyes open, I began to see a vision of something in the Spirit. I saw a huge group of teenagers, fifty to sixty thousand, in a stadium worshiping God. I saw them being sent into the nation as balls of fire. [Keep in mind that Dutch Sheets had no idea that Lou Engle would announce The Call D.C. that night.] God said, 'I will do a work in the youth of America. They will be a catalyst for the revival that I am about to bring.'"

Dutch, who contributes a chapter of his own to this book, continued, "In January God began to talk to me again. God said this is the hour for Washington. I am about to do a work that people will not believe. I'm going to take back the capital of the nation. I'm going to come with such a visitation that people will be coming to D.C. I'm coming with fire to burn out the corruption and the idolatry. I'm on a mission to pour out my Spirit in that city and the whole nation is going to sit up and take notice. I'm going to invade the White House, the Senate, the House, and every other agency there."

"This is the Night!"

After some other things, Dutch concluded by saying, "This is the night when God has taken the nutcracker. God said that by His sovereign plan and will, He brought together a group of people on this very day to fulfill what was spoken by the prophets. I believe that it's a new day. I believe that it's the hour for the capital of this nation, and I prophesy to you that revival is coming to Washington, D.C. We cry out to You, we plead with You, oh Man of War. Stir up Your zeal! Let this be the day. Remove the reproach off our nation's capital. Come now. In Your wrath remember mercy. We ask You for grace; not for what we deserve. Let a spirit of repentance and revival be released.

"We prophesy to Washington D.C.: repentance and cleansing from evil and unrighteousness. There is hope! There is another breath of God coming. We prophesy revival and repentance, life, conviction, miracles, the raising of the dead, spiritually and physically. We prophesy salvation in the Senate chambers. Sovereign, unplanned prayer meetings in the Senate, in the White House. We prophesy that the tunnel is now completed. Your heavenly coup is under way. We prophesy that it will go from D.C. into the nations. Arise, shine!"

Repenting for the Past
to Open the Future

As this historic meeting concluded, Tommy Tenney led the congregation in a prayer of repentance to former Mayor Marion Barry on behalf of unjust judgments against Washington D.C. Cindy Jacobs of Generals of Intercession called the youth present at the meeting up to the platform with adult leaders kneeling before them and repenting for their lack of faith that God would use their generation to turn our nation around.

The U.S. election of 2000 is now history. Few who have eyes to see will doubt that God's hand was upon our nation during the process. As I mentioned at the beginning, it seems clear that God had designed a prophetic tapestry, assigning many of His faithful apostles, prophets, and intercessors key roles in accomplishing His purposes. This book highlights some small pieces of that divine tapestry. Large numbers of other servants of God also heard His voice and were just as obedient to their Master as the ones you read about here. All in all, however, the body of Christ came to a new level of prophetic intercession in this season, and consequently the future looks bright for our nation!

Chapter Four

How a Prophet Sees Governmental Change

Chuck D. Pierce

Chuck D. Pierce is a widely recognized prophetic voice and leader in
the worldwide prayer movement. He
serves as vice president of Global
Harvest Ministries in relation with
the World Prayer Center, and as
president of Glory of Zion International Ministries in Denton, Texas.
Chuck coordinates prayer for many
of the major spiritual events and gatherings around the
world, and also serves as assistant coordinator of the U.S.
Strategic Prayer Network along with Cindy and Mike
Jacobs.

Throughout the ages, God has used prophets to help establish governments here on earth. He assigns them the task
of establishing a divine plumb line so that His people will
know how to pray correctly. It is His desire that the governments on earth will reflect His righteousness in heaven.

Isaiah 9:7 says: "Of the increase of His government and
peace there will be no end, upon the throne of David and over

His kingdom, to order it and establish it with judgment
and justice from that time forward, even forever. The zeal
of the LORD of hosts will perform this."

The Emerging
Apostolic Prayer Movement

Over the past decade, I have been privileged to work with
many ministries in mobilizing thousands of intercessors
for strategic prayer for the harvest. Part of this involved
establishing the World Prayer Center in Colorado Springs
with Peter and Doris Wagner. After our involvement in
mobilizing prayer for the 10/40 Window during the 1990s,
it became obvious that we needed to make a significant
shift so that intercessors could network more efficiently in
their focused prayer assignments. As a result, we now see
an emerging apostolic prayer movement that has the
strength, authority, and anointing to call forth change in
earthly governments.

How is the global prayer movement going to emerge
into prominence in the future? In a recent article in *Global
Prayer News,* Peter Wagner describes "10 Major Prayer
Innovations of the 1990s." He notes that the change in the
course of prayer throughout the church has actually
changed the course of the world. Innovations such as
identificational repentance, strategic-level spiritual warfare,
on-site praying, and spiritual mapping have stamped an
indelible mark on the progress of the prayer movement.
The advances made through these prayer innovations, and
others like them, have become the basis for how we con-
duct effective spiritual warfare.[1]

Church Government is Changing

Over the past several years we have watched God's govern-ment arise in the earth. That government is described in Ephesians 4:11 as including apostles, prophets, evangelists, pastors, and teachers. I believe that as the government of the church began to change, authority began to rise in the earth realm to change governments on earth. The role and gift of the apostle is becoming more prevalent in the leadership of the church today. With the rise of the New Apostolic Refor-mation and our newfound recognition of the gift and office of apostle, the church is coming into a new level of authority. Apostolic authority, combined with the essential role of the prophet, is allowing us to mobilize intercession with incred-ible results.

How do these leadership roles work together? Prophets are those who are called to mobilize the church to wield God's intercessory sword on earth. Intercessors pave the way for God's glory to be seen and His will to be established. Apostles execute God's will in the earth realm and establish His gov-ernment. Pastors maintain the field, so evangelists can bring in the harvest from each territory, nation, tribe, and tongue into the storehouse.

The Church and the Kingdom

So, who are we? What is "the church"? Many people con-fuse the church with the kingdom of God. However, they are not the same. The Kingdom is the overall divine purpose that includes the church. The church exists to see the Kingdom established and operating on earth. The church facilitates the

Kingdom. The kingdom of God is in conflict with the kingdom of Satan and the church operates as the armed forces of God in that war.

The Greek word for "church" is *ekklesia*, which means gathered to accomplish something or a group of people called out. The first time the notion of church was used in the Bible was when the children of Israel came out of Egypt. They were "called out" in order to move into God's inheritance that He had promised their forefather Abraham. This promise had been passed on to Isaac and on to Jacob. Then the promise moved from the place of fulfillment down into a foreign land, the land of Egypt. This had been prophesied in Genesis 15. However, to bring complete fulfillment of God's purpose, you must be at the right place at the right time. So even though the promise had stayed in Egypt for 400 years it had to be "called out" at God's perfect time so that His people could move forward and eventually fulfill their destiny.

Travail for a New Government

In *The Future War of the Church*, Rebecca Sytsema and I said this: "What did God do to call out His promise from one place and send to its place of fulfillment? First of all, we see that He changed governments over the people. 'Now it happened in the process of time that the king of Egypt died. Then the children of Israel groaned because of the bondage, and they cried out; and their cry came up to God because of the bondage. So God heard their groaning, and God remembered His covenant with Abraham, with Isaac, and with Jacob. And God looked upon the children of Israel, and God acknowledged them'" (Exod. 2:23-25).[2]

Notice that travail was produced in the heart of God's children of promise. And as they travailed God remembered His covenant blessing and promise that were resting upon them. This "calling out" is the beginning point for recognizing God's heart to mobilize His people for war. After God had chosen Moses and Aaron as His leaders, the Bible says, "This is the same Aaron and Moses to whom the Lord said, 'Bring out the children of Israel from the land of Egypt according to their armies'" (Exodus 6:26). In other words, the governmental order of the family clans permitted them to receive the promises that God had ordained for them.

I AM CONVINCED THAT [THIS] DECLARATION, ALONG WITH MANY OTHERS LIKEWISE PRAYING AND DECLARING THE WILL OF GOD, WAS INFLUENTIAL IN SETTING THE COURSE FOR OUR NATION OVER THE NEXT 40 YEARS.

God called the children of Israel out of Egypt because His desire had been to govern them Himself. He had His own ways to govern them in order to accomplish His purposes. In Exodus 18 we see that the Lord spoke to Moses through his father-in-law, Jethro, and gave him the strategy of governing the people through a network of judges and rulers who were responsible for a manageable number of people and who were ultimately answerable to God. Moses set up this God-given system of government which worked well for generations.

But then there came a time when the people wanted to be ruled by a king and they began to drift from God's pattern of government. Despite prophetic warnings from Samuel, they insisted and the Lord reluctantly gave them Saul. Right off the bat Israel got into real trouble with Saul. And then because Saul didn't have the heart to obey God in all his ways, their problems grew even worse. It would have been better for Israel to stick to God's governmental plan for them.

A New Authority

What can today's church learn from Israel's experiences? God's way has always been the best way to go. He has a way to govern, a sovereign plan which He has clearly spelled out for us. The first time the word "church" (*ekklesia*) is used in the New Testament is in Matthew 16:18-19, when Jesus says, "And I also say to you that you are Peter, and on this rock I will build My church, and the gates of Hades shall not prevail against it. And I will give you the keys of the kingdom of heaven, and whatever you bind on earth will be bound in heaven, and whatever you loose on earth will be loosed in heaven."

The context of these verses is a warning to the disciples to beware of the Sadducees and Pharisees. In those days, they held the keys of knowledge of the Scripture and, therefore, they had the authority to control the people through their understanding. But they had become corrupt and had lost the ability to gain God's revelation through the Scriptures that they knew so well. As a result, they became legalistic and harsh and began actually to hinder God's work on earth rather than accurately reflecting God to His people. We see Jesus' frustration with them once again in Luke 11:52 when He says, "Woe to you lawyers! For you have taken away the key of knowledge. You did not enter in yourselves, and those who were entering in you hindered."

When, in Matthew 16, Peter confessed that Jesus was the Christ, the Lord transferred the keys of knowledge and kingdom authority from the Sadducees and Pharisees to His disciples and He breathed on them and He said, "now take this all over the earth." That same authority has been delegated to the church today. *We* are now the ones responsible to draw people into the Kingdom. We have the keys to do this whether we ever choose to use them or not.

A New Government

As the fledgling church struggled to gain its footing, God used the apostle Paul to bring necessary order and governmental understanding. God was once again giving a pattern of government in which He would delegate His authority to certain individuals, much as He did with Moses and Aaron and the judges and rulers of the Old Testament.

As I have mentioned, the pattern for this government is found in Ephesians 4:11-13 which says, "And He Himself gave some to be apostles, some prophets, some evangelists, and some pastors and teachers, for the equipping of the saints for the work of ministry, for the edifying of the body of Christ, till we all come to the unity of the faith and of the knowledge of the Son of God, to a perfect man, to the measure of the stature of the fullness of Christ." This pattern is again echoed in 1 Corinthians 12:28, "And God has appointed these in the church: first apostles, second prophets, third teachers..."

According to these passages, this pattern was meant to extend beyond the first century. Otherwise, Paul would not have included the phrase, "till we all come to the unity of the faith and of the knowledge of the Son of God, to a perfect man, to the measure of the stature of the fullness of Christ." In the two millennia that have passed since these words were written, the church has not yet reached these goals. We still

need equipping of the saints for the work of ministry and edifying of the body—which means, we still need apostles and
prophets!

Apostles, Prophets, and Intercessors Work Together to Unlock God's Purposes of Government

Through the prophets, prophetic revelation will be released
for strategies to unlock the harvest fields that have been held
in captivity for many, many years. The Lord said in Matthew
16:18 that He would give us the keys of the Kingdom. Apostolic leadership with a heart for harvest and an understanding
of the times is beginning to arise throughout the earth. At
every major turning point in the history of the church, the
Lord has called forth leadership that understand His time and
methods for advancing His Kingdom. Intercessors are beginning to receive the burden of God for harvest in an increased
intensity. God always begins by communicating His heart to
those who will stand in the gap and pave the way for His
glory to come to earth.

Supernatural communications from heaven are now connecting with the earth realm more than they have for a long
time. This was a key in the U.S. election of 2000. Apostles
and prophets have always worked together in biblical history
to usher in key moves of the Spirit of God. There is an unprecedented connecting between these two governmental gifts
that is releasing vision and setting an order for harvest. Strategic, prophetic intercessors who know how to break through
the powers of darkness are connecting with the apostolic leadership that God is raising up.

God Releases Prophetic Words into the Atmosphere over Territories

Once the word of God is released through prophecy, it is never forgotten. It is stored in heaven until God is ready to release it back into the earth. In the election of 2000, I believe God brought an understanding to the prophets that this was a key *kairos* time, and that we were to seize the opportunity, and move forward into the future of this nation with victory!

1. Tallahassee, Florida

As I look back to the election of 2000, I see how God began to set a course to change the atmosphere over Florida before election day came in November. You will see some of the detail of this in Bill Hamon's chapter, "Sealing Tallahassee."

In late 1998 I received a call from Martha Lucia, the prayer leader for Christian International. During our conversation, she said this: "Tallahassee will become the high place of our nation." My mind said, "Why Tallahassee?" But my spirit bore witness with the anointed prophetic word she was speaking.

Biblically, we find that during the time of the judges, Israel had adopted the pagan custom of offering sacrifices at high places (elevated hilltops). The pagans believed the closer they were to heaven, the greater the chance their prayer and sacrifice would reach their gods. So these high places were usually linked with Baal worship. From these high places, Satan developed a plan and a throne of iniquity in a territory. These high places caused worship to be deviated from God and would allow dark forces to stay in place that could send an entire nation astray. So again, why Tallahassee as a "high place"?

On the Steps of the State Capitol

I didn't have to understand. We just began to pray and mobilize. I found myself in Tallahassee three different times before the election. In one of those times we ended up on the steps of the State Capitol with approximately 300 intercessors praying for the state of Florida and its relationship to our nation. This was in April of 2000, long before the election.

Do you see how prophetic intercession operates? Moving out by faith, we were beginning to legislate the heavens over a state governmental power that would turn out to be the determining factor for the future government of our whole nation. After election day, Florida became the "State of War" for our nation. Tallahassee was the central battlefield. You can read more about this in other chapters in this book. I believe that without the prophetic declarations that had been going on for almost two years and the resulting travailing prayer, our nation would have missed this crucial window of opportunity. The U.S.A. would now be moving in an ominously different direction.

2. West Palm Beach, Florida

In September 1999, Global Harvest Ministries had planned a conference in West Palm Beach, Florida. This conference was cancelled, but I was invited to go anyway to hold a meeting with the intercessors of that region at Bishop Harold Calvin and Prophet Brenda Ray's 4000-member church, Redeemed Life. During this time, a major hurricane had targeted that part of the East Coast. The hurricane threatened to cancel my flight, but just in time it turned northward enough so that I was able to fly from an engagement on the 700 Club to West Palm Beach. Through this, the Lord let me know that He was opening a special window of revelation. This caused me to be especially alert to the voice of God as I ministered there.

Once I arrived there, the Lord began to speak an unusual phrase to me. He said that this city would be known as "Metheg Ammah." I found that this came from 2 Samuel 8:1: "After this it came to pass that David attacked the Philistines and subdued them. And David took Metheg Ammah from the hand of the Philistines." In Hebrew "Metheg Ammah" means "the bridle of the mother city." What is this? God was saying that the bridle of the Philistines was to be placed in David's hands, and then they would be under his power.

This began to speak to me in a powerful way as soon as I arrived in West Palm Beach. I perceived that it had to be one of those times when God was poised to transfer authority from heaven to His government on earth. Therefore, I taught on the Philistines and the process that David had to go through in order to overcome them. At the end of this message, the Spirit of God fell on the whole congregation, and He began to speak.

The "Bridle Mother City of the Nation"

The Lord began to say that West Palm Beach would become the "Bridle Mother City" of our nation. Just as the bridle in the mouth of a horse can turn it in one direction or another, West Palm Beach and Palm Beach County would be the bridle that would set the course of the nation's direction. I didn't understand what that meant. Certainly, no one there was re-lating it to the election of 2000, still more than a year away. However, the Lord went on to say that all eyes of the world would turn toward this city.

God then even specifically said "*Go back 125 years* and you will find the pattern of iniquity that you are up against to turn this nation." The Spirit of God fell in that room. From that day forward, the intercessors stayed alert, researched, gained understanding, and warred all the way through until the election process in this "Bridle Mother City" was resolved and our nation was turned. As history has now confirmed, all eyes of the world were indeed turned toward West Palm Beach as the election was being disputed. When researching the 125 years the intercessors found that during the election of Rutherford B. Hayes, Palm Beach County and West Palm Beach had also become the national focal point in that election dispute!

3.   Camarillo, California

Before the election, Global Harvest Ministries was holding a conference on the Apostolic Church Arising in Camarillo, California. This gathering had leaders from all over California. During that conference, God had me speak out this prophecy:

"I am going back to 1962 in this nation and to the things that occurred in 1962 bringing an infirmity upon this nation. I would say to you I am raising up an apostolic strength and an apostolic government in My church that will have the power to break that infirmity. Certain things have happened since 1962 that have caused a spirit of infirmity to cause My people to be bowed low and the destiny of this nation to take a wrong turn. But I say to you I am even right now beginning to shift and release an anointing into certain individuals in this land that can cause the power of that infirmity to break.

"Those weaknesses that entered into the DNA structure of

this nation in 1962 I am about to expose, I am about to send, and I am about to break off this nation. ...Go back to what occurred in the media in 1962 and you will see how to break the cycles of weaknesses that have been implanted in this land ... an anointing has been released and I have chosen to release that anointing in California and what brought infirmity into this nation – I say the apostolic leadership in California will cause it to be reversed."

California Will Be the Turning Point

God went on to say, "This state is going to be the turning point of this election in days ahead [I take that to mean the revelation that was at that moment being released at this conference]. I've brought you here. I've anointed you. I'm saying to you before you leave here, make a prophetic declaration concerning which direction the nation needs to go. ...Do not leave here until you say, 'This nation will go this way!' When you make that declaration, which I've put in your mouth, it's going to take action in this state. I gathered this remnant together this week because if you had not gathered, this nation would have gone in the wrong direction."

Let's look at this. What was this prophecy saying? I believe it meant that if these apostles, prophets, and intercessors from California would go forth to raise up apostolic leadership and prayer throughout that state, there would be a change in the entire nation. And how this state raised up apostolic leadership would be a precursor for what needed to happen throughout our nation from state to state. As the church comes into new apostolic leadership, the civil government of our nation will also change.

We also connected this back to Washington D.C. Attending the Camarillo conference was a key pastor from D.C.,

David Freshour. He was brought up on stage and I said, "How you go back and declare from this conference is how our nation will go." We then made prophetic declarations and sent him and his wife, Maureen, back into the capital of our nation. It's amazing how God does this. He produces an anointing in one territory and then sends it like an arrow into the heart city of an entire nation. The Freshours went back and began to pray new and fresh for our nation out of the revelation that was released in California. California then mobilized prayer and 600 teams went throughout the state praying for the change of our nation.

Moving from "Praying" to "Saying"

As several have mentioned, it was very difficult for us to declare publicly who God's choice was in this election, even though we knew. However, the Lord had impressed me several years prior of that which He had in mind for General Colin Powell after his retirement from the military. God had showed me specifically that Colin Powell would be positioned in the U.S. government. As the year 2000 progressed, I began to see that for Colin Powell to be in his divinely-chosen place, George W. Bush would also have to be positioned properly. Furthermore, I began to see prophetically the will of God for Dick Cheney for such a time as this. Even though I knew all of this very clearly, I was reluctant to speak it out.

However, it is important to move from a place of "praying to saying." In other words, we must move from our intercessory closet to make intercessory declarations that will set God's purposes in motion here on earth. This happened when during the meeting of the Apostolic Council of Prophetic Elders (ACPE) on November 28, 2000. Although it was three weeks after election day, the election had yet to be decided. It was as if in that meeting the Lord said, "Declare what is to be!" As one we came together in agreement that George W. Bush, Dick Cheney, and Colin Powell would be positioned for the future of our nation.

How important was this? I am convinced that the ACPE declaration, along with many others likewise praying and declaring the will of God, was influential in setting the course for our nation over the next 40 years.

Notes

[1] C. Peter Wagner, "Looking Back to Surge Ahead," *Global Prayer News*, Vol. 1, No. 3, July-September, 2000, pp.1, 12.

[2] Pierce, Chuck D. and Rebecca Wagner Sytsema. *The Future War of the Church* (Ventura CA: Renew Books, 2001), p. 66.

Chapter Five

Sealing Tallahassee

Bill Hamon

Bill Hamon is the co-founder (along with his wife, Evelyn) and president of Christian International Ministries in Santa Rosa Beach, Florida, home to an undergraduate and graduate School of Theology. His 40-plus years of ministry experience provide a balanced, biblical approach to the restoration of the office of the  prophet. Bill Hamon is respected by church leaders around the world as a senior leader of the prophetic company God is raising up in these last days.

I n the late 1990s we at Christian International (CI) in Santa Rosa Beach, Florida received a prophetic word that we were to begin intense intercessory prayer for our state. I immediately knew that, as the apostle over Christian International, it was up to me to cast the vision and set the direction for obeying God and implementing His assignment. I met with my major leadership team, Tom and Jane Hamon, co-pastors of our central church, and our intercessory prayer minister, Martha

Lucia, in order to seek God for the first steps in fulfilling the prophetic word.

The Holy Spirit began to impress upon us that whatever happened in Florida would have an effect upon the whole nation. In those days, of course, we had no inkling that the U.S. election of 2000 would be decided by Florida's electoral votes. What we did know, however, as a result of the experiences of many years in prophetic ministry, was that when God gives us a clear word of prophecy, He expects us to go into action with the weapons we have learned to use in the spiritual realm. This is exactly what we did, knowing that in some sense or other, in ways yet to be determined, the outcome of our spiritual warfare here at home could help establish the future of our country.

The River Flowing from Pensacola

We started the process by doing the spiritual mapping type of research we had learned from George Otis, Jr., and others. We needed to know how to target our intercession. Before moving out we agreed it was important to know exactly how God would have us pray for our territory so that breakthrough and revival could come to this area. We were sure that He had a divine strategy for us to follow.

Word had come to us that in 1989 it had been prophesied publicly that a tremendous outpouring of the Holy Spirit and revival would occur in the Pensacola area. One of our CI ministers, Jim Wies, who was living in the Phoenix, Arizona area at the time, attended the meeting and reported that the prophet suddenly stopped his teaching and asked, "Is there someone here who is from the Pensacola, Florida area?" Jim Wies was just making preparation to move to De Funiak

Springs, a city near Pensacola, to begin pastoring a church there, so he stood up to receive the word of the Lord.

Another prophetic word came through David Yonggi Cho who said that God had shown him clearly that there would be a mighty outpouring of His Spirit in Pensacola and that it would eventually flow like a river eastward across the panhandle to the East Coast, travel up the East Coast and then engulf the nation. On Father's Day in 1995 the powerful Brownsville Revival broke out. Brownsville is a part of greater Pensacola, apparently the headwaters of God's river of revival that would flow forth.

The Panhandle—
A Spiritual Gateway

As we began to pray and do more research we found that Pensacola is the oldest continuously settled colony in the entire United States. We discovered that it was settled by the Spaniards in 1559 and that it pre-dates any settlements in the northeast sector of our nation which we normally believe to be the foundations of our nation. Then we noticed that directly east of Pensacola on the Atlantic Ocean is St. Augustine, the oldest continuously-occupied city in the continental United States, founded in 1565. (Pensacola was unoccupied for a few years.) It had by then become obvious to us that the panhandle area of Florida, with Pensacola on the west and St. Augustine on the east, represented an important foundation of our nation from the perspective of Western civilization. We believed that the panhandle of Florida was, indeed, a spiritual gateway to our nation and that it would be vital for us to engage in strategic prayer and spiritual warfare in order to open this gateway in the spirit so that God's move for spiritual revival and reform could take place.

Since Tallahassee, the capital of Florida, is located right between these two key cities, it is in the center of the panhandle portion of Florida. We prophetically felt that Tallahassee was to be the physical place for the divinely-ordered prayer initiative. At that point we still weren't sure of our exact strategy, but we continued to seek the Lord regarding what He desired to accomplish through us. We were convinced that a spiritual breakthrough in Tallahassee would bring breakthrough for our entire nation.

Canceling the Assignment of Hell

On May 19, 1997, I was in Tallahassee recording a program at the Christian television station. After filming, a team of intercessors accompanied me to the state capitol building at midnight. The filming crew came with us to the observation floor at the top of the 22-story building. I then began to pray and prophesy over the state of Florida. This is what God showed me:

"We declare right now that we cancel the assignment of hell to hold back the judicial system and the government in this place; and we say the kingdom of God is going to arise and the purpose of God is going to be fulfilled. ...As the saints war here on earth, the angels are going to war in the heavenlies and we are going to see godly government begin to be set up over this state and over this nation. ...This state is a gateway into the nation. It is a gateway for many things, but we close the gate to the devil and we open the gate to the righteous. ...We decree right now that the assignments of everyone who is legislating, voting, bringing in evil and unrighteousness, and causing trouble in this state are canceled. We decree now that they will make the right decisions on crucial matters which can affect the destiny of our state and nation."

In March, 1998, Chuck Pierce, one of America's most respected prophets, came to minister at a conference at our Christian International headquarters. Not knowing anything about what we had done, Chuck began to prophesy to us about taking our territory here in the panhandle of Florida. He said that breakthroughs that we would have here would bring breakthrough for many others. He said, "This is a key territory. ...As this place unlocks, your destiny will begin to unlock in a new way. Pray for this area that your destiny will be unlocked to see the church advance. ...As the church, we are in a precarious place, over the next few months, because God is attempting to impart a new mantle of intercession and give us the authority to cause our territory to turn around. He is training us right now to be a legislator of His justice."

We were deeply moved and challenged by this confirming word from the Lord. Through the rest of the year, the Lord's direction as to how He wanted us to proceed was becoming clearer.

Target: Tallahassee

Early in 1999 we felt the Lord's strategy was for us to saturate Tallahassee with strategic prophetic intercession. We were to gather as many other pastors, leaders, and intercessors as possible to move with us in what we were sensing God was saying. They were to come from as wide a spectrum of the body of Christ as possible. Jo Ann Arnett from the Tallahassee Bible Institute helped us coordinate our first meeting time. We reserved a hotel banquet room and had a meal catered to feed

250 people. We sent letters to all the churches and those from our combined mailing lists, not sure how may would actually show up. As it turned out, we had almost 285 people come to that first meeting in May of 1999. It was standing room only. Those in attendance came from various churches and reflected a variety of denominational and ethnic backgrounds. Chuck Pierce flew in for this meeting and taught the group on how to take our territory through strategic prayer. At that time we built a solid, united base for fulfilling our prayer assignment for the city. The strategy was now becoming clear. All were very excited!

GOD HAS POSITIONED HIS MAN IN THE SEAT OF GOVERNMENT, AND HIS CHURCH IS ALSO POSITIONED TO CONTINUE TO LEGISLATE FROM THE HEAVENLY REALM THOSE THINGS WHICH ARE TO TRANSPIRE ON EARTH.

Later that year we convened another gathering in Tallahassee. This time we met in a church and there were approximately 250-300 in attendance. Again, Chuck Pierce flew in and laid more foundations for us through his teaching and demonstration of taking territorial dominion through unified, strategic prayer.

During this meeting Chuck gave a very interesting prophetic word. He said that the eyes of the nation would be drawn to the state of Florida and upon Tallahassee. He further prophesied that God was going to use the Florida State University football team to draw the eyes of the nation to Tallahassee. Sure enough. Florida State ended up winning the National Championship later that year!

The High Place of the Nation

In April of 2000 Christian International convened a gathering of intercessors which we called "The High Place of the Nation" Conference, believing that spiritually and foundationally Tallahassee represented a high place that needed to be taken for the Lord. Chuck Pierce returned and joined me in ministering along with Tom and Jane Hamon, Martha Lucia, Jo Ann Arnett of Tallahassee Bible Institute, and Chip Bueller of Morning Star Church in Tallahassee. This was a strategic time of releasing the apostolic/prophetic foundation-laying anointing for this city and our nation.

On Saturday morning the entire group from the conference, including the worship team with all their instruments, gathered on the steps of the capitol building for a key time of repentance, prayer, praise, and prophetic proclamation. A number of Tallahassee pastors were vital participants in this powerful time of prayer. Emphasis was made time and again through the word of the Lord regarding the connection of Tallahassee with Washington, D.C. The prophets and intercessors saw clearly that as breakthrough happened here in Florida, the ripple effect would be felt in our nation's government.

When we concluded we felt as though we had accomplished our spiritual task. Though there would obviously be a need for ongoing strategic prayer in Tallahassee, we knew that we had just done something that would affect the destiny of our nation.

Once the election was over some months later, it had become clear to us that much of our intercession, prophetic declaration, and spiritual preparation had been for the purpose of paving the way for the proper resolution of the electoral process, assuring that the man of God's choosing would occupy the White House for the next four years.

All Eyes on Florida State

We had little previous inkling that the eyes of the nation, even the eyes of the entire world, would come to rest upon Florida during the election of 2000. As a matter of fact, on November 27, 2000, *Sports Illustrated* magazine came out with a cover which had the words "Decision 2000: All Eyes Are on Florida (State)" comparing the political race to a football national championship. The word of the Lord surely came to pass.

As a result of faithful, obedient prophetic intercession, we are now positioned and ready to reap the spoils of our warfare, on a local level as well as nationally. God has positioned His man in the seat of government, and His church is also positioned to continue to legislate from the heavenly realm those things which are to transpire on earth.

Chapter Six

The Cali-West Palm Beach Connection

Héctor Torres

Héctor Torres is the president and founder of Hispanic International Ministries, a member of the Apostolic Council of Prophetic Elders and the Spiritual Warfare Network in Latin America, and is the author of several Spanish and English books. As a result of his ministry of networking pastors and teaching about intercession,  spiritual warfare, and city transformation, Hector has traveled in North America, Latin America, Southeast Asia, Scotland, and Norway.

Ever since George Otis, Jr. of The Sentinel Group released the widely-acclaimed *Transformations* video in 1999, the city of Cali, Colombia has become well-known around the world for its all-night prayer vigils and the unique unity among the evangelical churches and leadership of that city. What the video does not say, however, is the process by which that city entered into a "transformation" mode.

It is interesting that the rest of this story in Colombia played a prophetic role in the U.S. election of 2000. Let me explain.

A Battalion of Intercessors in Cali

History began to be molded for Cali, Colombia, through the ministry of prophets and intercessors. In 1984 a group of Brazilian intercessors from the Lydia Women's Association was praying for Colombia. The Lord clearly spoke to them at that time about how He was going to raise up a battalion of intercessors in Cali, Colombia that would change the destiny of the nation of Colombia.

Before then, in 1979, Randy and Marcy MacMillan began to intercede for the city of Cali and the nation of Colombia. They began to raise and train teams of intercessors to pray and develop intercessory strategies that would help them tear down the strongholds of violence, corruption, greed, and drug trafficking in what has been described as the "most powerful crime cartel in the world."

During those years the Lord led them to enter into what is now known as "strategic-level spiritual warfare" and "prophetic intercession." Many of the things they did were not at that time common church knowledge or practice, such as going to the high altars of demonic power and repenting for the iniquities and curses brought upon the land by the idolatry and violence of the former inhabitants of the region.

Mapping Cali

As part of their strategy, they took a map of the city of Cali and divided it into seven different areas. As a part of this spiritual mapping, they began to ask the Lord to reveal to them the strongholds of darkness prevailing in each one of these areas. After they received what they believed to be revelation from God they would send intercessors to pray on site in those areas and to bind the strongman who was holding that territory in captivity.

In 1991, C. Peter Wagner and I were invited by the Colombian National Pastors Association and the city of Bogota pastors' association to teach the first spiritual warfare seminar in that nation. At that conference, Randy and Marcy MacMillan invited me to visit Cali and do a seminar on the same topic. This was in April of 1992, while I was a pastor at Word of Grace Church in Mesa, Arizona.

Given the novelty of the topic, it was not surprising that the support and participation of the local pastors' association was minimal. Many pastors did not believe in spiritual warfare, nor was there any meaningful unity among the local pastors and other Christian leaders of the city. However, the MacMillans were persistent and they continued to host an annual prayer, intercession, and spiritual warfare seminar. I was generally invited to be one of their conference speakers. As the years went by, opposition diminished and the local pastors became more open.

God's Prophetic City to the Nations

On one occasion, the Lord gave me a powerful prophetic word for the city of Cali. The prophetic word was that Cali would be known as God's prophetic city to the nations. Out of Cali the Lord would send prophetic worship and prophetic intercession and Cali would be known for its prayer and praise. It was not until four years later that things began to change. In April of 1995 the city of Cali hosted a Praise and Worship Convocation and over 20 thousand people attended. This was the beginning of what are now known as the Cali Prayer Vigils.

Although the *Transformations* video seems to imply that Pastor Julio Ruibal's martyrdom was the primary cause of Cali's spiritual revival, those who labor in the city know that there was more to it than that. A covenant of unity was made at Ruibal's funeral, but it was not immediately implemented. It took the deaths of two other pastors, each death taking place exactly thirty days after the other, for the pastors of Cali to bow before the Lord and repent for their disunity and self-centeredness. Each one of the pastors was silently asking if they might be number four! Roosevelt Muriel, the president of the pastors' association, states: "We all asked the Lord, what was it that He wanted us to do? God's answer was that He desired that his church come into oneness that the world would believe in Jesus."

Roosevelt Muriel didn't know it at the time, but God was preparing a prophetic role for him in the U.S. election of 2000.

A City Desired of the Nations

At the 1996 Cali Prayer Vigil, the Lord gave me a prophetic word for the city and for the nation of Colombia. Coming from the text of Isaiah 60:10-17, the word highlighted the promise that foreigners would come to build and to visit and the city would no longer be called desolate but desired of the nations.

It was the following year that the MacMillans invited Cindy Jacobs and Bill Hamon to hold the First Prophetic Conference for Cali. This conference laid a foundation for establishing the prophetic calling of the city.

I then invited Roosevelt Muriel from Cali to participate in what we called "The 2000 Prayer Quake" in Phoenix, Arizona. Muriel went from Phoenix to speak in Stuart, Florida. There he met some people from nearby Palm Beach County who paved the way for Roosevelt to use his gift of prophecy to help determine the course of the U.S.A.

An American Fire
Ignited in Florida

While in Stuart, Muriel accepted an invitation to West Palm Beach for a series of meetings in August of 2000. Pastors and other Christian leaders came together to hear the report that Muriel was bringing from Cali about unity. Many different churches, denominations and races were included. On that occasion Roosevelt and his wife, Betty, prophesied that *"they saw a little fire starting to burn in the map of the USA and it started in Florida and it burned up the map of USA. They said it was like that map of Bonanza that burned the land."*

Muriel returned to West Palm Beach in October, less than a month before the U.S. election, to do a meeting with pastors from Palm Beach, Martin, St. Lucie, and Indian River Counties. About 250 pastors attending a luncheon heard Roosevelt's remarkable prophecy: *"The eyes of the nation and the world will be upon West Palm Beach. What is going to happen here will affect the whole nation and eventually the whole world."* He also told them

...OUR STRATEGIC-LEVEL PRAYERS IN CALI PLAYED SOME PART IN DISPLACING THE EVIL FORCES OF DARKNESS THAT WERE BATTLING IN THE HEAVENLIES TO CONTROL AMERICA'S FUTURE.

that, as spiritual leaders of the region, they had divinely-delegated power either to stop what God wanted to do, or to allow the coming circumstances to alter the course of the nation in the direction that God desired.

Soon after this came the now-famous counting of the votes in Florida and in particular West Palm Beach and Palm Beach County. Television cameras from around the world were crowded into West Palm Beach. Before the election was decided, some church leaders from West Palm Beach attended a conference in Cali. I was there, and I led over 5000 people in fervent prayer for West Palm Beach and for the United States. We knew prophetically that these prayers were essential for God to intervene on behalf of the United States. We felt that our strategic-level prayers in Cali played some part in displacing the evil forces of darkness that were battling in the heavenlies to control America's future.

The word of prophecy, followed by faithful and obedient intercession can truly determine the course of nations! This is the way that God has chosen to order His universe.

Opening the Door to the White House

Dutch Sheets

Dutch Sheets serves as senior pastor of Springs Harvest Fellowship in Colorado Springs, Colorado. He is an instructor for Christian Life School of Theology, and is the author of the best-selling book *Intercessory Prayer.* Dutch has traveled extensively, teaching throughout the United States, Canada, Central America, Africa, and much of Europe. Dutch's current ministry thrust focuses strongly on restoring godliness to America.

Author and lecturer Leo Buscaglia once talked about a contest he was asked to judge. The purpose of the contest was to find the most caring child. The winner was a four-year-old child whose next-door neighbor was an elderly gentleman who had recently lost his wife. Upon seeing the man cry, the little boy went into the old gentleman's yard, climbed onto his lap and just sat there. When his mother asked him what he had said to the neighbor, the little boy said, "Nothing, I just helped him cry."[1]

Three and a Half Intense Hours

On Wednesday, October 4, 2000, a month before the U.S. election of 2000, God somehow powerfully touched my heart with His, and I felt like that little boy. For three and a half hours God allowed me to help Him cry over our nation. It would be impossible for me to exaggerate the emotional and spiritual depth of the prayer burden I was given. As I felt God's aching heart for America, I thought my own would break in two. During those agonizing three and a half hours, I wept harder and from deeper within me than I ever knew was possible.

One of the results of this incredibly strong burden that the Lord placed upon me was a decision to issue a national call to prayer for the upcoming presidential election. I knew that the communications infrastructure was by then in place through the U.S. Strategic Prayer Network (USSPN) which could ultimately transmit the word to huge numbers of people. I followed the protocol and checked the word out with Peter Wagner and Chuck Pierce. They agreed that the message needed to be sent out to the widest circle without delay. It turned out that, within 24 hours, no fewer then one million individuals had this document in their hands, and many entered into travailing intercession.

The Letter to Intercessors

The following is a portion of that letter:

"There must be a turning in this nation toward righteousness, and this will only happen if God's man is elected into office. It is not so much that this man is now ready spiritually to take the nation where God wants, but rather that he has a heart upon which God can effectively move. I believe that if the election were held today, God's purposes would not be established. (I am not basing this on polls or debates, but solely on what the Lord revealed to me that night.) In fact, the results would be such that His purposes for this nation would be set back for many, many years – possibly decades.

"During this intense time on Wednesday night, God led me to Daniel 10 where the account is given of great warfare in the heavenlies between the forces of darkness and light. He showed me that the outcome of the current battle regarding this election will be determined by the prayer of the Church. If there is enough prayer and fasting, God's person will be elected, righteousness will prevail, and God's plan will be established. On the other hand, if there is not enough prayer, God's person will lose the election and the turning of this nation will be drastically delayed.

Is This Presumptuous?

"I realize that what I am about to say could sound presumptuous, but I believe God witnessed to my heart that one of the greatest prayer efforts in the history of our nation must be mobilized immediately. The amount of prayer that would normally be done for the election is absolutely not enough. I have never before attempted something such as this, but after seeking confirmation from trusted national leaders in the Body of Christ, I believe the Holy Spirit earnestly desires that I issue a red alert regarding the seriousness of this hour.

"I am asking for those who agree with me that this warning is from the Lord to intensify their prayer efforts by doing several things:

• Incorporate significant amounts of prayer into church services. Perhaps turn some entire services (Wednesday nights, Sunday nights, even Sunday mornings) into times of intercession for the election. If not entire services, at least give major blocks of church meeting time to prayer.

- Additional prayer meetings, both day and evening, be orchestrated for this purpose.

- A national fast be held during the last 21 days before election day. (This would begin October 17th and continue through November 6th.) Prayer meetings on each of these 21 nights are needed.

"Daniel 2:21 states: 'He changes the times and the seasons; he removes kings and raises up kings; he gives wisdom to the wise and knowledge to those who have understanding.' This can and must happen. It will come to pass, however, only if we heed this imperative call to intensified, fervent prayer.

"If you agree with the urgency of this message, please pass it on to your contacts and ask them to do the same. Let us unite in this cause and see God turn our nation back to Him."

Responses from Around the World

A number of other Christian leaders either heard similar warnings from the Lord, or bore witness to mine, and sent the alert to their constituents. We received hundreds of responses from around the world (not just from America). I was a guest on The 700 Club, at their request, three different times to trumpet these alerts. Newspapers and magazines called, radio stations did interviews. From what we could tell, hundreds of thousands, if not millions, of Christians around the world responded with regular and intense prayer.

Three weeks later I sensed that some weariness might be settling in. God also seemed to intensify the burden within me. Consequently, I sent a follow-up alert on October 31. Here is part of that communication:

The Follow Up

"Thank you for your overwhelming response to the 'Prayer Alert For This Nation.' **However, we must not let up at this critical point. I am extremely concerned as we enter into this last week before election day. We are in danger of apathy and fatigue keeping us from faithfully interceding until the end.** We cannot stop; we have not yet prevailed in this endeavor. There is a great, great urgency that we intensify our intercession during this last week. It is not a time to decrease and let down our guard because we're approaching the finish line. Rather, it is a time to press forward with even greater strength to see the goal accomplished. Once again, I am asking: *Please intercede for this election!*

- Pastors, please hold daily prayer meetings in your churches and devote time for prayer during your regular services.

- Church members, please give this alert to your pastors and plead with them to call their people together for concerted prayer for the election.

- I am strongly encouraging that from Wednesday, November 1, through election day, Tuesday, November 7, 24-hour prayer chains be put into effect.

- Also, I believe that we must continue to fast in whatever

form the Lord leads during these critical days, and, if possible, do a water-only or juice-only fast Sunday through Tuesday."

An Undecided Election

The crucial significance of this prayer alert and the level of warfare over the nation became extremely obvious when, after the election, the identity of the next president had not yet been determined. There were many times in the ensuing weeks when it looked as though the outcome could go either way.

As the body of Christ responded, God answered the fervent prayers of His faithful intercessors. I believe He gave us the president that He desired America to have. God is obviously neither a Republican nor a Democrat. This election was not essentially about a political party, but about finding a person whom God could use to accomplish His purposes for the nation. In ancient Israel, God could not do what He wanted through King Saul, so He looked for a man after His own heart. That person, of course, was King David. I believe that a similar thing happened in this election. We obeyed the prophetic word, God heard our prayers, and He graciously gave us a man after His heart to lead our nation.

IF WE CONTINUE TO DILIGENTLY AND CONSISTENTLY HEAR GOD, OBEY HIM, AND PRAY INTO BEING WHAT THE SPIRIT IS SAYING TO THE CHURCHES, WE CAN SEE AMERICA TURN BACK TO GOD.

I realize that there are sincere believers who would disagree with me. For one thing, it is clear that certain minorities, especially in America, feel their cause is much safer in the hands of Democrats. I respect that position and I understand the passion behind it in the hearts of many brothers and sisters. Nevertheless, in this particular historic moment, I simply believe it was absolutely imperative that God have someone as our president who is very open to Him and who walks in righteousness. To me, the entire ordeal was never about Republican or Democrat.

What We Learned

The Lord taught me several important things during this unforgettable election prayer season. One was a greater understanding of how to carry a prayer burden, especially one of this magnitude, entirely by the power of the Holy Spirit, not my own. At one point, I actually asked the Lord to release me from this burden. Knowing this was a literal war in the heavenlies for the soul of America, the emotional weight was simply more than I thought I could bear.

However, the Lord refused to release me from the assignment. He reminded me that I must not carry the burden in my emotions, but rather my spirit. Actually, I believe I entered into an entirely new level of revelation of this spiritual principle, which I am sure will play a very important role in my future ministry.

Unity in the Body

I also saw as never before the value of cooperation and unity in the body of Christ. If God had not been establishing the communications infrastructure through the global prayer movement during the past decade, I don't think we would have been able to accomplish what we did. The following examples show the crucial roles these had during this season of intercession.

- I sought confirmation from other spiritual leaders on the accuracy of the burden, as well as how to communicate it.

- Many leaders, key ministries, and thousands of people helped to distribute the alert.

- Pastors incorporated much more prayer than usual for the elections into their services and into the overall lives of their churches.

- In Florida, where the battle was so intense, churches, leaders, and intercessors joined together in an unprecedented way. Their unity and perseverance were superb.

Our Spiritual Authority

A final truth that God impressed strongly on me during this process of prayer had to do with our spiritual authority as believers. Shortly after receiving this burden, God began a remarkable series of confirmations to teach me this. It was the most amazing series of personal confirmations that I have ever received, reinforcing to me the fact that God was indeed speaking to me about our nation.

★ On a cross-country flight, I happened to notice that my departure time was 2:22, I then was seated in row number 22 and the total travel time was 2 hours and 22 minutes. My first thought was, *What a strange coincidence!* Then the Lord reminded me that He had been speaking to me about the election from Isaiah 22:22, "I will place on his shoulder the key to the house of David; what he opens no one can shut, and what he shuts no one can open" (NIV). *Would God do something like this to bring me confirmation?* I wondered.

★ A couple of days later I received a phone call from Sam Brassfield, a spiritual father in my life. While in prayer, Sam had felt the Lord prompt him to call and give me Isaiah 22:22, emphasizing the phrase, *the key of David.* He said, " Dutch, God is giving you a key of authority in this nation."

★ Soon afterward, I went to Washington D.C. on a ministry trip, and there a trusted intercessor friend of mine gave me a gift at the meeting. She said the Lord had impressed her months earlier to buy it for me, with the instruction that He would let her know when to give it to me. It was a beautiful silver key, and her words to me were, "This is the key of the city!"

★ Another man, knowing nothing about this, came to me after that meeting with three keys and said, "This morning I felt impressed to bring you these three keys." He, too, realized they symbolized spiritual authority. Matthew 16:19 states, "And I will give you the keys of the kingdom of heaven, and whatever you bind on earth will be bound in heaven, and whatever you loose on earth will be loosed in heaven."

★ A week later I was in San Diego with Chuck Pierce. Chuck told me that God had led him to give me a key. He had been given this key in New York by people who said it represented a revival anointing for America. Chuck said,

"The Lord impressed me to give it to you."

★ After that service, another man gave me three more keys, saying he had been impressed by the Lord to do so. Incredibly, the number "222" was on each of these keys!

★ A couple of weeks later I was in California again to meet and pray with my friend, Lou Engle. Lou said to me, "God has been speaking to me about Isaiah 22:22. I've even had dreams about the number 22 and this verse. And at a meeting I did recently, the number of my hotel room was 222."

★ I came home from that meeting, shared this with our church and a young man in our congregation said to me, "Just today God directed me to Isaiah 22:22. I felt it was a verse for the church."

★ Another lady in the service had been awakened from a dream at 2:22 a.m. and heard the Lord speak to her about those numbers.

★ Still another lady in the service, a visiting pastor's wife from New England, had also had a dream the previous night. In her dream there was a man with an old set of keys. She asked him, "What are you doing with those?" He replied that he was going to throw them away because they were just old keys. In the dream she said to the man, "Please don't throw them away. They are precious. May I have them?" He then gave her the keys.

Over the course of a few weeks, I had no less than 25 remarkable confirmations that God was speaking to me about keys of authority and relating this to Isaiah 22:22. He was clearly saying, "I am giving you authority – keys – to impact the nation."

Though the occurrences were happening to me, I realized the word was not just for me, but for the entire body of Christ. We truly have been given keys of authority from God to legislate from the heavenlies, opening doors that can't be closed by Satan or any person, and closing doors through which evil and destruction might otherwise enter.

The White House Door is Opened!

On December 2, after so much confirmation and prayer, I became convinced that it was time for an extremely bold act of prayer and prophetic declaration. I, along with two other people, went to the White House grounds late that Saturday night and, standing at one of the gates, began to pray Isaiah 22:22 along with Psalm 34.

We first prayed for then Vice President Al Gore and his family. We blessed him in numerous ways and asked God to fulfill the destiny He had designed for him. We then, however, spoke out, took the authority of the keys, and spiritually closed the door of the White House to him, decreeing that he would not enter there to lead this nation.

We then proceeded to decree that the door to the White House was open to George W. Bush, and that he would enter it as the president of the United States. This intense prayer time lasted about 30 minutes.

Presumptuous? Arrogant? Some would no doubt feel that it was. However, by that time I was thoroughly convinced God had confirmed again and again that we had this authority in the spirit and that we were to exercise it. I was willing to obey God even if it might look foolish to others. Agreeing with the prayers of millions of people that presumably by then had been stored in the heavenly prayer bowls mentioned in Revelation 5, we simply made the declarations that turned out to be the final release. A few days later, the Supreme Court made its decisive ruling and Vice President Gore conceded.

Praying In the Future

As Beth Alves underscores in the next chapter, we must not stop praying for America. However, we now have a starting point of hope for the future that we did not have before the election of 2000. I believe there was an enormous breakthrough in this presidential election attributed, by those who have eyes to see, to the prayers of an obedient church. I would not be surprised if a new direction has been set in place which will last for at least forty years. If we continue to diligently and consistently hear God, obey Him, and pray into being what the Spirit is saying to the churches, we can see America turn back to God.

What a blessing this will be for the future generations!

Notes

[1] Jack Canfield and Mark Victor Hansen, *A Third Serving of Chicken Soup for the Soul* (Deerfield Beach FL: Health Communications, Inc., 1996), p. 12.

Chapter Eight

What Has Been Gained by Intercession Must be Maintained by Intercession

Beth Alves

Beth Alves is founder and president of Intercessors International in Bulverde, Texas, and is a faculty member of Wagner Leadership Institute and Christ for the Nations Institute. She is known for her teaching on prayer and prophetic ministry, and has taken small groups on strategic prophetic intercession missions to the White House and into many nations. Beth supports spiritual leaders around the world in prayer by teaching intercessors to pray for them on a daily basis.

Dreams come and dreams go in my life and I usually don't remember them once my feet hit the floor. However, in August of 2000, I had an unusual dream that set in motion a new direction in my life and in the ministry of Intercessors International, of which I am president.

When I awoke the dream still seemed so together, so real. Immediately, I told it to my husband and then carried it in my heart and through intercession for days.

A New Prayer Mandate

What made this dream so different? It added a new prayer mandate that would bring a change to our ministry and directly impact the president of the United States through prayer. About a month later, I began sharing this dream with a friend, who is also a member of our board of directors. He actually started crying and interrupted, "I can finish the dream for you. I had almost the exact same dream myself!"

The dream started with a knock at my door. When I answered the door, I saw a boy was standing in front of me holding a pair of men's dress shoes in his hand.

In the dream, I instantly *knew* that he was 10 years old and that the number ten meant the redeemed, the church, but I also *knew* that the boy represented the Holy Spirit. Even though he was young, His face had the features of a Hispanic male about 30 years of age. While I looked into His clear blue eyes it was like looking back into eons of time.

There was a knowing, even in my dream, that the features of this young Hispanic man represented Jesus. Without a doubt, the ancient look in His eyes was that of the Father.

"George W. Bush Has Been Elected President"

As soon as the door opened, the young boy said to me, "George W. Bush has been elected president of the United States."

Turning around, and with great excitement, I called out to a room full of people, "Hey, Bush has been elected president!" A shout of jubilation went up from those in the room. I turned back to the young man standing in front of me and he said,

"President George W. Bush wants to see you."

Surprised, I looked up and saw the president and Laura, the first lady, standing across a river that ran in front of my home. They were surrounded by Secret Service agents. The president and his wife smiled and waved at me. I waved back.

Carrying Shoes to the White House

While I was waving, my attention was diverted back to the boy as he placed the men's dress shoes in my hand. He said, "These belong to President George W. Bush and my Father wants you to carry them into the White House."

I remember thinking, "He can't be the president's son because the Bushes have twin daughters." As though the boy perceived my thoughts, he repeated the same phrase again. With that he turned and ran toward the president.

Holding the shoes, I shut the door with my foot and thought again, "But Bush has twin daughters." Once more I heard the same words, "These belong to President George W. Bush and my Father wants you to carry them into the White House." With this, I fell to my

IN PRAYER,
THE MORE GROUND
YOU GAIN,
THE MORE YOU HAVE
TO MAINTAIN,
AND THE MORE YOU
MAINTAIN,
THE MORE YOU HAVE
TO GAIN.

knees and cried out, "Oh! Father! It is you!"

It was then that I realized that this multi-aged young man not only had something to do with the church, but He also was symbolic of the Godhead. I woke sobbing, not only in my dream but also in the natural.

I knew this dream had come from the Lord, but I didn't know what it meant and I found myself constantly meditating on it. I couldn't get it out of my mind. I had questions and God had answers!

Authority from a Higher Power

One evening several days later, I went to sleep praying and pondering, once again, on what those shoes meant. In the morning, my husband turned on the radio and I heard the person speaking say, "And now to conclude my message on shoes..." This caught my attention. He went on to say, "Remember, when shoes are on a man's feet they mean *peace*. When they are off the feet it means *that a man has given up his authority to a higher authority*." To support his teaching, the speaker proceeded to give the scriptural references.

Instantly, I realized that the Lord had commissioned me to carry the President's shoes into the White House. But how? I still did not know! So, I continued to pray.

While interceding for him, in the theater of my mind, I would hold up a pair of men's dress shoes and pray that President Bush would give up his authority to a higher authority: the Lord God of heaven and earth.

During my times of intercession, I came to understand that the multi-age of the young man in my dream was not only representative of the agelessness of the church, but also of the Godhead. In my spirit, I knew that the Lord was calling the church to a fresh commitment to pray for the health, welfare, and protection of our president, that all might go well with us as a nation.

Dutch Sheets' Prayer Alert

As the days passed and it was getting closer to the election, a prayer alert for our nation was issued by Dutch Sheets calling the church to a national fast. This was to be carried out over the last twenty-one days just prior to the election.

As I read Dutch's e-mail, I inquired of the Lord, "How do you want me to fast?" The answer came deep within, and the words came emphatically to me, "Fast as you choose, but don't fast now! Start after the election and fast for 40 days." This really startled me! I could not imagine why. Thanksgiving, maybe? Could there be danger, etc., etc.? I had all sorts of questions at that moment that were left unanswered, but I knew it was the Lord, so I set my heart in that direction.

It wasn't until the day after the election that I began to realize what my assignment was. I now understood that carrying those shoes had to do with praying for President Bush and his walk in the office of president of the United States and his walk as a Christian.

Our Nation's Destiny

Even though I was praying for the president, I knew that our nation hung in a balance. I knew that the days ahead would not be easy and that the course of our nation's destiny for a long time to come would be determined by decisions that would be made during George W. Bush's time in office.

I continued to pray that he would learn to relinquish his authority to God's authority in order that the Father's will be done in this nation. There was a knowing that he will have to make major decisions concerning Israel, and that his decisions would ultimately have a worldwide effect.

During this time, I had become aware that my commission was not just the daily prayers that I prayed for Mr. Bush, but it was also to raise up an entire ministry of prayer strictly for the president, his family, and the Secret Service agents who guard them. It was then that I began to understand the symbolism in my dream of the young boy and why his age would be representative of the church. This was not just for me but for the body of Christ as well.

The President's P.I.T. Crew

The Lord began to unfold a plan and out of that God birthed a new facet of Intercessors International that we call *The President's P.I.T. Crew.* The acronym P.I.T. stands for **P**ersonal **I**ntercession **T**eams. Personal does not mean that we are in personal contact with the president, but that our commission is to pray for the issues that concern him personally. This idea was taken from that of a pit crew for a race car driver. The role of a pit crew is to see that every need of the driver and his or her race car is met with readiness and speed—refueling, repairs, and maintenance—in order to win the race. The job of The President's P.I.T. Crew is to pray for the personal needs of President Bush, his family, and those who guard them as he runs the race set before him.

Through prayer and intercession, I have gained the knowledge of what the Lord wanted of me; and what He meant by carrying the President's shoes into the White House, but I lacked the wisdom of details. Continued intercession brought continued results and many more to help. I knew that it would be a costly endeavor but with prayer and obedience I knew that it could be done.

God's Provision Comes

For a starter, we needed someone to oversee this ministry with the help of Intercessors International's dedicated staff. It wasn't long before the Lord sent a woman with the gift of intercession and a call to help develop The President's P.I.T. Crew.

God sovereignly provided three rooms for offices rent free in a church and then someone else totally refurbished the rooms. Computers, furniture, and a telephone system were given to Intercessors International to help develop this new phase of the ministry. This all happened within a few weeks.

At one of the Global Harvest Ministries conferences, the vision was shared about The President's P.I.T. Crew. Within two weeks we had approximately 800 people who had expressed desire to partner with us in praying for the President. The number continues to grow daily. God is raising up state and regional coordinators to give oversight. Churches and prayer groups nationwide are becoming involved.

With the wonderful world of technology much of the communication can be done through e-mail on a weekly basis. Where people do not have access to e-mail, monthly updates are being sent. It is our goal to have people praying twenty-four hours a day, seven days a week.

Helping People Pray

Many people desire to pray, but they don't know how. To

meet this need, Intercessors International provides trained and qualified instructors to do a variety of prayer seminars to help people understand and practice prayer, intercession and how to hear the voice of God.

We also have a book called *Daily Prayers* that provides Scripture prayers to pray, and other resources to help with this endeavor. A website is also available to keep intercessors current and focused all that is happening with The President's P.I.T. Crew.

It is exciting to see a dream become a reality! What God has done, is doing and what is yet to come is still unfolding, but one thing for sure, *what has been gained by prayer must be maintained by prayer* in order to bring glory to God and complete the race set before us.

Always remember:

In prayer,
The more ground you gain,
The more you have to maintain,
And the more you maintain,
The more you have to gain.

Chapter Nine

How to Pray
the Future into Being

Chuck D. Pierce

Throughout history, we can discern an interesting pattern. There is a clear pattern of relationship between God's timing, changes of political leadership, and release of new revelation.

God Removes Kings and
Raises Up Kings

For example, we find this in Daniel 2:20-22: "Blessed be the name of God forever and ever, for wisdom and might are His, and He changes the times and the seasons; He removes kings and raises up kings; He gives wisdom to the wise, and knowledge to those who have understanding. He reveals deep and secret things. He knows what is in the darkness and light dwells with Him."

This is a tremendously important principle for the church to understand. The Greek word, *kairos*, is the word used in the New Testament to describe the opportune or appointed time that God has set for something to occur. Jeremiah knew the *kairos* time for purchasing a certain property as a prophetic act (see Jer. 32:6-44). Jesus knew the *kairos* time for beginning His ministry—and the *kairos* time for returning to Jerusalem to be crucified. It is also necessary that we understand that God has *kairos* times—appointed seasons—for certain things to occur, and we must respond in prayer when He tells us to press into those opportunities. The seasons are changing, and we must be willing to change with them and move as the Spirit of God leads us in order to seize the *kairos* opportunities at hand! If we don't, God's best for whoever is involved will not come to pass.

Changing Governments and Nations

How does this relate to governments and nations?

Hannah wanted a baby. (The story is found in 1 Samuel 1-4.) Therefore, she travailed before the Lord until she became pregnant. This was not just a child who would satisfy her motherly desires. This child was to represent the change in an entire earthly government and determine the future of the nation of Israel. This child would prophetically transition the earthly kingdom of Israel into proper alignment for God's Kingdom blessings. Hannah's travail brought the conception of God's purpose to earth that ultimately changed a government. Without her travail we can only conjecture what might have happened.

Another example is found in 1 Kings 17-19. Here we find the story of Elijah the prophet. Elijah declared that the heavens would cease from giving rain. This was not just to bring drought to a land, but to convince the corrupt earthly govern-ment that God had supreme authority over them. He then confronted the earthly false religious systems that were con-nected to and controlled by the government. He cried for God to disconnect their demonic, idolatrous power from the earth. God backed him through a public power encounter. Elijah then legislated the heavens through prayer, travail, and pro-phetic declaration at God's ordained (*kairos*) time to produce rain. This was to convince the nation that the drought was a result of the corruption of the earthly government headed by Ahab and Jezebel. This gave the nation an opportunity to break ties with the seduction of Baal worship that this gov-ernment had aligned with.

Jesus was constantly in conflict with the societal structure of that time. He had come not only to change people's hearts, but also to redeem them from Satan's grasp. The religious system of the time was unable to perceive this change. The government was in complete alignment with the religious sys-tem of the time. Therefore, Jesus would always warn His disciples to "beware of the Pharisee and beware of Herod." Jesus said, "If you had known, even you, especially in this your day, the things that make for your peace!" (Lk. 19:42-44). Then the Lord gave a list of things that would happen to them because they did not know the time of their visitation. Understanding timing (*kairos*) is very important. As we rec-ognize the timing of God and respond accordingly, entire nations can change.

How God Sets His Time (*Kairos*) in America

As the election of 2000 was approaching, I happened to be

doing a conference in Oklahoma. Oklahoma is probably the most mobilized state for prayer in our nation. However, Oklahoma has also gone through great tragedies over the last six years. John Benefiel, pastor of Church on the Rock in Oklahoma City, has been used as an apostle to align pas-

tors and intercessors across the state. Over the past five years we have had quarterly meetings in Oklahoma.

AS WE RECOGNIZE THE TIMING OF GOD AND RESPOND ACCORDINGLY, ENTIRE NATIONS CAN CHANGE.

Most of our quarterly Oklahoma meetings are concentrated on the needs of the state. However, sometimes the Spirit of God comes down in one of those meetings and gives revelation pertaining to the whole nation. Here is a portion of one of those words that was released on October 27, 2000. We were in an incredible place of worship and through a word of wisdom I saw Isaiah 32. I opened my Bible, read the chapter out loud, and while I was doing it the Lord began to speak to me. Keep in mind that this revelation came during the intense time of prayer that our nation was in for the election of 2000.

I saw Isaiah 32 and the Lord began to speak to me: "I am setting My course for judgment upon the states of this land. …Judgment will come based upon the complacency of the church from state to state to state. For you have thought judgment would come based upon the acts of the national government that is now in place but I would say to you that, instead, judgment will come because of the complacency of

My people.

"Remove false judgments for I am setting a new course of righteousness. Those that I am about to put into places of authority need to be surrounded with your shields of faith. I long to cover them so that a righteousness can be seen that has not been seen before in this land. Therefore, they must stay shielded so that they might display My righteous judgments.

"War will now break out in these next 18 months. This will be a war of great spiritual magnitude. The war will be over the boundaries of the future, for the enemy has shifted boundaries. There is a war over the justice of this land. I will establish justice in the midst of My people. Therefore there will be war over laws that have been established wrongly. Know that you are warring with an antichrist system. Therefore, do not fear this supernatural war that I am calling My people to be engaged in."

This word was given with leaders present from a seven state region. The mood of the Lord was one of encouragement and His voice released an awareness of His character of justice and order. When this word was given it was also sent out to intercessors in the U.S. Strategic Prayer Network across the nation. The word was given to mobilize people to pray now to determine the future of our nation.

How, Then, Shall We Pray?

For some time my predominant role in the body of Christ has been to use my apostolic anointing to mobilize prayer worldwide. As I have done this through the years, I have identified some prayer points that I believe are necessary to go with this word given in Oklahoma. God wants us to build a wall of fire and protection from city to city and state to state throughout our land. Keep in mind that prophecy is usually given in order to stimulate aggressive intercession.

Before you begin to pray, define the boundaries within which you are praying. Paul says, "[God] has determined their preappointed times and the boundaries of their dwellings" (Acts 17:26). Some of you will be praying for your home with the following prayer points. Others of you will pray for your church. Some of you are called to pray for your city. Some have been extended a call from the Lord to pray for your state. And then, of course, it is very important to pray for our nation. However, for the prayer points below I will use your city and state as points of reference.

1. **Ask God to remove complacency from your life and region.** Complacency stops and distorts vision. Therefore, pray that the power of complacency will be broken, for example, from your church and from your city. Sometimes the enemy sends a spirit of slumber. So declare that a spirit of slumber is broken off the church in your region. Shout, "Awake!" when you are driving throughout your city. Allow that word to go through the spirit realm of your city and state.

2. **Ask the Lord for the spirit of grace and intercession to fall on your city and state.** Many times we have not, because we ask not. If the intercessors will cry out for the spirit of grace and intercession, God will begin to blanket the people of your region who have never felt the burden to pray. We will see communion and prayer begin and changes will be activated. You will probably begin to hear of a spirit of travail coming forth in people throughout your city and state.

3. **Pray for the key authority structures in your city.** Ask the Lord to put an urgency in the gatekeepers. Cry out for mercy for the gatekeepers who are now operating in unbelief. Ask for a sweeping gift of faith to fall upon spiritual authorities in your region.

4. **Ask the Lord to build up the wall with the correct spiritual leadership for your city, region or state.** God raises some up and He puts others down. Don't pray from a motivation of control, but release "leadershift" powerfully into the spirit realm and watch this take action in your region. Trust God to work in His timing.

5. **Cry out for corporate worship times to arise in your city, state, and region.** Pray that not only will 24-hour prayer and worship be established, but declare that there will be corporate worship times where the church gathers just to worship a holy and living God. Pray that what has happened in Cali, Colombia (see Chapter 6) will happen in your city as well. True worship tears down idolatrous structures.

6. **As a new level of worship is established in the church in your city, ask the Lord to break the power of child sacrifice and close down abortion centers.** Ask the Lord for true worship to overthrow powers in the heavenly realm that are influencing earthly actions contrary to the will of God such as abortion. Ask the Lord to raise up state gatherings where people come from all over the state to worship. I see gatherings very much like Promise Keepers, but they will be "state owned" by the apostles, intercessors, prophets, pastors, and spiri-

tual leaders of that region. Stadiums will be filled with
people worshiping the living God.

7. **Ask for lawless structures that are linked in with terrorist activities to be revealed.** This word was given in
   Oklahoma where the worst terrorist attack on U.S. soil
   occurred. Declare that all the hidden evil structures that
   are governed by false religious principles will be uncov-
   ered.

8. **Ask the Spirit of God to empower the church with a
   new coat of armor for spiritual war.** Declare, as we
   operate with the weapons of spiritual warfare, that unjust laws that have been established will be overturned.
   This is a day of Esther overturning Haman's decrees.
   Pray that the right judges will be put in place from region to region to region.

9. **Ask the Spirit of God to penetrate dead, religious
   structures that are resisting His move in your city
   and state.** Declare that those who are speaking out of a
   mind that resists the Holy Spirit will be silenced and
   that the Spirit of God will begin to break out in various
   places in your city and state. The Spirit of God is the
   restraining force that stops demonic powers from ex-
   panding their evil works in your region.

10. **Do not fear, but cry out for God's perfect restorative
    grace to take action throughout our entire nation.**
    Even though this word mentions judgment, it gives very
    clear instruction that judgment does not have to come if
    the church will rise from complacency now and wor-
    ship!

Now is the Time to Pray the Future into Being

It is my prayer that you will allow this and other prophetic words to bring you into a new expectation of the victory that God has prepared for the church in days ahead. This is a *kairos* time for God's people to understand authority, for authority is the key to power. This is a time for us to deal with the spirit of fear that has imbedded itself into the heart of the church. The spirit of fear creates an unsound mind, it weakens power, and it negates love.

God has given us an awesome responsibility. Through the prophets, He has shown us, and continues to show us, His holy desire for the future of our nation. But, as we see through history, God makes the fulfillment of His desire contingent on the obedience of His people. Apostles, prophets, and intercessors play a crucial role. If the apostles, acting on the word delivered through the prophets, effectively mobilize the intercessors, and if the intercessors, in turn, enter into powerful, strategic, prophetic intercession, we in the body of Christ will truly be praying the future into being. It will be God's best future for us, and our nation will be blessed as never before.

Subject Index

A

Aaron, 47, 49
Abraham, 33, 46
Acts 17:26, 98
Ahab, 95
Alves, Beth, 84, 85-92
Amos 3:7, 13, 20
apostles, 45, 50, 101
Apostolic Council of
    Prophetic Elders, 8, 14-
    15, 32, 56-57
apostolic prayer movement,
    44
Arnette, Jo Ann, 63, 65
Augustine, 9

B

Baltimore, 31, 32, 33
Barry, Cora Masters, 37
Barry, Marion, 37, 41
Basinger, David, 10, 16
Bass, Christian, 21
Benefiel, John, 96
Bethel College, 10
Bethel Temple, 33
Boyd, Gregory, 10-11, 16
Brassfield, Sam, 81
breaker anointing, 32
Bridle Mother City, 53-54
Brownsville Revival, 61
Bueller, Chip, 65
Buker, Diane, 22-23, 29

Burke, Edmund, 26
Buscaglia, Leo, 73
Bush, George W., 8, 9, 12,
    13, 23, 56-57, 83, 86-90
Bush, Laura, 87

C

Cali, 67-72, 99
Cali Prayer Vigil, 69-70
California, 54-56
Call D. C., The, 38, 40
Calvin, Harold, 52
Calvin, John, 9
Camarillo, CA, 54-56
Campbell, Darla, 21
Campbell, Ron, 21
Canfield, Jack, 84
Celebration of Discipline, 16
Cheney, Dick, 56-57
children of Israel, 46-47
Cho, David Yonggi, 61
Christian International, 22,
    51, 59, 65
Christianity Today, 16
2 Chronicles 20:20, 13
Church on the Rock, 96
Clinton, Bill, 27
Colombia, 67-72, 99
Colombian National Pastors
    Association, 69
1 Corinthians 12:28, 49

D

Daily Prayers, 92
Daniel, 25-26
Daniel 7:9-10, 21
Daniel 10, 75
Daniel 10:12-13, 25-26
Daniel 2:20-22, 93
Daniel 2:21, 76
David, 53, 78
Dawson, John, 29
Democrat(s), 12, 18, 78-79

E

ekklesia, 46, 48
Elijah, 94-95
Elijah Prayer, 38-39
Engaging the Powers, 16
Engle, Lou, 35, 38-39, 40, 81
Ephesians 2:20, 14
Ephesians 4:11, 13, 45
Ephesians 4:11-13, 49
Ephesians 4:13, 13
Esther, 100
evangelists, 45
Exodus 2:23-25, 46
Exodus 6:26, 47
Exodus 18, 47
Ezekiel 22:30, 18

F

Florida, 19-20, 29, 22-25, 52, 59-66, 80
Florida State Capitol, 52, 62-63
Florida Supreme Court, 20, 23, 25
Florida U.S. Strategic Prayer Network, 22, 29

Foster, Richard, 8-9, 16
Freshour, David, 56
Freshour, Maureen, 56
Future War of the Church, The, 46, 57

G

Generals of Intercession, 17, 41
Genesis 15, 46
Genesis 26, 33
Global Harvest Ministries, 20, 43, 52, 54, 91
Global Prayer News, 44, 57
Glory of Zion International, 43
Glory Tabernacle, 36
God at War, 10-11, 16
Gore, Al, 12, 23, 83, 84

H

Hamon, Bill, 22, 59-66, 70
Hamon, Jane, 59, 65
Hamon, Tom, 59, 65
Hampton, VA, 33-36
Hanley, Jack, 39
Hannah, 94
Hansen, Mark Victor, 84
Harvest Rock Church, 38
Hasker, William, 10, 16
Hayes, Rutherford B., 54
Healing America's Wounds, 29
Hess, Tom, 29
high places, 51-52, 65

Hispanic International Ministries, 67
Hitler, Adolph, 22
Holocaust, 29
Howell, Rees, 16

I

identificational repentance, 19, 24, 29, 44
Immanuel's Church, 37
intercession, governmental, 17-29
intercession, prophetic, 10, 41, 68, 101
intercessors, 45, 50, 101
Intercessors for America, 22
Intercessors International, 85, 90, 92
Intercessory Prayer, 73
International Strategic Prayer Network, 29
Isaac, 33, 46
Isaiah 9:7, 43-44
Isaiah 22:22, 81-83
Isaiah 29:4, 24
Isaiah 32, 96
Isaiah 60:10-17, 70
Israel, 90

J

Jacob, 46
Jacobs, Cindy, 17-29, 41, 43, 70
Jacobs, Mike, 43
Jeremiah, 94

Jeremiah Project, The, 21
Jesus, 94, 95
Jethro, 47
Jews, German, 22, 29
Jezebel, 95
Johnson, Ron, 32, 36-37

K

kairos, 51, 93-94, 95, 101
1 Kings 17-19, 94-95
Kooiman, Brian, 29

L

Lucia, Martha, 22, 51, 59-60, 65
Luke 11:52, 48
Lydia Women's Association, 68

M

MacMillan, Marcy, 68-70
MacMillan, Randy, 68-70
Mall, The, 38-39
Maryland, 33-34, 37
Matthew 6:10, 20
Matthew 16, 48-49
Matthew 16:18, 50
Matthew 16:18-19, 48
Matthew 16:19, 81
Metheg Ammah, 53
Ministries of Compassion, 37
Morning Star Church, 65
Moses, 47, 49
Muriel, Betty, 71
Muriel, Roosevelt, 70-72

N

National Prayer Committee, 22
New Apostolic Reformation, 45
"Nutcracker Prophecy," 33-34

O

Oklahoma, 96, 100
Openness of God, The, 10, 16
openness theology, 10-11
Otis, Jr., George, 60

P

pastors, 45
Pensacola, 60-61
Pharisees, 48
Philistines, 53
Pierce, Bart, 31-41
Pierce, Chuck D., 22, 29, 43-57,
    63-65, 74, 81-82, 93-101
Pinnock, Clark, 10, 16
Pisani, Dennis, 36-37
*Possessing the Gates of the
    Enemy*, 29
Powell, Colin, 56-57
prayer, 11-12
President's P.I.T. Crew, 90-92
Progressive Vision, 29
Promise Keepers, 38, 99
prophecy, 24, 51
prophecy (specific words of),
    33-34, 40-41, 54-55, 62-63,
    64, 69, 71, 96-97
prophet, gift of, 14
prophet, office of, 14
prophetic activity, 24
prophets, 13-15, 45, 50, 101
Psalm 24:7-10, 24

Psalm 34, 83
Psalm 75:6-7, 24

R

Ray, Brenda, 52
Redeemed Life, 52
Republican, 12, 18, 78-79
Revelation 5, 84
Rice, Richard, 10, 16
Ridings, Rick, 32-34, 38-
    39
Rock City Church, 31, 32
Ruibal, Julio, 70

S

Sadducees, 48
Samuel, 47
1 Samuel 1-4, 94
2 Samuel 8:1, 53
Sanders, John, 10, 11-12,
    16
Satan, 51
Saul, 47-48, 78
Secret Service, 90
Senate, 40-41
Sentinel Group, 67
Sheets, Dutch, 26-27, 35,
    39-41, 73-84, 89
shoes of authority, 87-88,
    90
Smith, Malachi Jude, 28
spiritual mapping, 60, 68
spiritual warfare, 10, 11,
    24, 44, 60, 61, 68, 69
Sports Illustrated, 66
Springs Harvest
    Fellowship, 39, 73

St. Augustine, FL 23-24, 61
St. Louis, 29
Sytsema, Rebecca, 46, 57

T
Tallahassee, 20, 22, 51-52, 62-65
Tallahassee Bible Institute, 63, 65
Tenney, Tommy, 32, 35-38, 41
Third Serving of Chicken Soup for the Soul, A, 84
Tidewater, VA, 34
1 Timothy 2:1-3, 18, 27
Torres, Héctor, 67-72
Transformations, 67, 70

U
U.S. Strategic Prayer Network, 15, 17, 21-22, 29, 43, 74, 97
United States Supreme Court, 8, 15, 20, 25, 84

V
Virginia, 33-37

W
Wagner, C. Peter, 7-16, 21, 29, 44, 57, 69, 74
Wagner, Doris, 44
Washington D.C., 27, 32-41, 55-56, 65, 81
Washington for Jesus, 39
West Palm Beach, 22, 29, 52-54, 71-72

White House, 40-41, 83-84, 87-88, 90
Wies, Jim, 60-61
will of God, 9, 18, 19, 21, 25-26, 40
Wink, Walter, 9, 16
Word of Grace Church, 69
World Prayer Center, 44
World War II, 16, 22

Z
Zechariah 8:16, 23